To: Avery

Be Blessed.

# NOBODY JUMPED OFF THE BOAT

## WE ARE ALL IN THIS TOGETHER

Second Edition

Live Blessed

### THIS IS A CONTINUATION OF THE JOURNEY BOOK SERIES

Stay Blessed.

By

## Reverend Dr. C. E. McAdoo

Foreword: Reverend Dr. Vincent Harris

Charlie Edward McAdoo

Concise Publishing
A division of Concise Consulting & Related Services
P.O. Box 55323
Little Rock, AR 72215

ISBN: 978-0-9862247-8-2

Unless otherwise noted, scripture quotations are taken from
The Message: The Bible In Contemporary Language (by
Eugene H. Peterson). Copyright (c) 2002

Concise Publishing February 2017


Printed in the United States of America

Cover design by Leron McAdoo
Backyard Enterprises

**Prayerfully Dedicated to:**

The Charlie & Odell Peyton Family and

The Thelma & Talitha McAdoo Family

## Acknowledgments

First and always, I thank the Lord. I thank my family for helping me understand the concept of relational living. I also thank my friend, Ivria Johnson, Jr., for his guidance as I wrote this. I also thank Dr. Jan Austin for editing this second edition of this work of faith. Her understanding, keen observations, and writing skills were invaluable.

I thank my daughter-in-law, Stacey, an accomplished author in her own right, for help with formatting. Special thanks to my wife, Gloria, and my children, Leron, Charlie II, and Madra, for their guidance and faith in my efforts. I also thank my daughter-in-law, Billynda, and my son-in-law, Johnathan.

I must also give thanks for my grandchildren, Norel, Jamee, Charlie III, Billy and Uel Noel. They are among my greatest blessings!

# CONTENT PAGE

# PREFACE

A preface is an introduction to a book, or a setting forth of the scope and purpose of what has been written. I want to model for the reader what I always tried to teach students during my time as an adjunct professor. To gain an of a writer's intention at the beginning of a book serves for better understanding. Also, what we read about relationships improves our understanding of others.

The purpose of *Nobody Jumped Off the Boat* is to share the story of Noah and the Ark he built, the families that joined him, and the animals that came from every species. It is quite remarkable in itself. I find the fact that none jumped off equally remarkable, and believe it proves a great deal. We know that different people bring different personalities. I think there had to have been some conflict within the Ark. There had to be differences in understanding, in morals. I use the story of Noah's Ark as a way to help us understand that it is possible for people of different persuasions to live together and to become better from doing so. Noah and others on the Ark had to get from one point to the other. The key to their journey and our own is understanding the dynamics within personalities, and the power struggles from the family to the church, the school, and the workplace, struggles that arise within any community.

In the midst of all within Noah's Ark, every person and every other living thing remained on the boat. One of the things I see in human relationships is that people often forget what enables us to get from one point to another. We must have some understanding that effective relationships are for our betterment if we are all to continue to be in this together. As Reverend Dr. Vincent Harris mentioned in his foreword, the *I* and the *mine* must turn into *we* and *us*.

Human beings are all part of that little hyphen in the middle, the one I will explain should you not have heard this before. This hyphen in the middle represents all that we accomplish between the date and year we are born and the date and year we die. The purpose of *Nobody Jumped Off the Boat* is to talk about what we do in that time of our life - that span represented by the hyphen - and how we build relationships with one another.

When we look at it theologically, there is no way that one race of people, social class, or gender can claim ownership of all. There is no way that one community of people or church can say that their faith, or their way of practicing it, is the only way. We are all in this together in our families, our churches, and our communities.

I offer the story of Noah's Ark as a framework only. It is my hope that Christians, non-Christians, and those who proclaim no religion will read this book. I use the Noah story because I think it will help each of us, whether we have read the Bible or not, to understand that we are often thrust into situations without realizing how those situations, and those who are with us, impact our personal growth and strength. As was the case for Noah and those who joined him in the Ark, we are all in this together.

## The Message: The Bible in Contemporary Language (by Eugene H. Peterson)

### Genesis 6:1-22

**1** When the human race began to increase, with more and more daughters being born, **2** the sons of God noticed that the daughters of men were beautiful. They looked them over and picked out wives for themselves. **3** Then God said, "I'm not going to breathe life into men and women endlessly. Eventually they're going to die; from now on they can expect a life span of 120 years." **4** This was back in the days (and also later) when there were giants in the land. The giants came from the union of the sons of God and the daughters of men. These were the mighty men of ancient lore, the famous ones. Noah and His Sons **5** God saw that human evil was out of control. People thought evil, imagined evil - evil, evil, evil from morning to night. **6**

God was sorry that he had made the human race in the first place; it broke his heart. **7** God said, "I'll get rid of my ruined creation, make a clean sweep: people, animals, snakes and bugs, birds - the works. I'm sorry I made them." **8** But Noah was different. God liked what he saw in Noah. **9** This is the story of Noah: Noah was a good man, a man of integrity in his community. Noah walked with God. **10** Noah had three sons: Shem, Ham, and Japheth. **11** As far as God was concerned, the Earth had become a sewer; there was violence everywhere. **12** God took one look and saw how bad it was, everyone corrupt and corrupting - life itself corrupt to the core. **13** God said to Noah, "It's all over. It's the end of the human race. The violence is everywhere; I'm making a clean sweep. **14** "Build yourself a ship from teakwood. Make rooms in it. Coat it with pitch inside and out. **15** Make it 450 feet long, seventy-five feet wide, and forty-five feet high. **16** Build a roof for it and put in a window eighteen inches from the top; put in a door on the side of the ship; and make three decks, lower, middle, and upper. **17** "I'm going to bring a flood on the Earth that will destroy everything alive under Heaven. Total destruction. **18** "But I'm going to establish a covenant with you: You'll board the ship, and your sons, your wife and your sons' wives will come on board with you. **19** You are also to take two of each living creature, a male and a female, on board the ship, to preserve their lives with you: **20** two of every species of bird, mammal, and reptile - two of everything so as to preserve their lives along with yours. **21** Also get all the food you'll need and store it up for you and them." **22** Noah did everything God commanded him to do.

**Genesis 7:1-21**

**1** Next God said to Noah, "Now board the ship, you and all your family - out of everyone in this generation, you're the righteous one. **2** "Take on board with you seven pairs of every clean animal, a male and a female; one pair of every unclean animal, a male and a female; **3** and seven pairs of every kind of bird, a male and a female, to insure their survival on Earth. **4** In just seven days I will dump rain on Earth for forty days and forty nights. I'll make a clean sweep of everything that I've made." **5** Noah did everything God commanded him. **6** Noah was 600 years old when the floodwaters covered the Earth. **7** Noah and his wife and sons and their wives boarded the ship to escape the flood. **8** Clean and unclean animals, birds, and all the crawling creatures **9** came in pairs to Noah and to the ship, male and female, just as God had commanded Noah. **10** In seven days the floodwaters came. **11** It was the six-hundredth year of Noah's life, in the second month, on the seventeenth day of the month that it happened: all the underground springs erupted and all the windows of Heaven were thrown open. **12** Rain poured for forty days and forty nights. **13** That's the day Noah and his sons Shem, Ham, and Japheth, accompanied by his wife and his sons' wives, boarded the ship. **14** And with them every kind of wild and domestic animal, right down to all the kinds of creatures that crawl and all kinds of birds and anything that flies. **15** They came to Noah and to the ship in pairs - everything and anything that had the breath of life in it, **16** male and female of every creature came just as God had commanded Noah. Then God shut the door behind him. **17** The flood continued forty days and the waters rose and lifted the ship high over the Earth. **18** The waters kept rising, the flood deepened on the Earth, the ship floated on the surface. **19** The flood got worse until all the highest mountains were covered **20** - the high water mark reached twenty feet above the crest of the mountains. **21** Everything died. Anything that moved - dead. Birds, farm animals, wild animals, the entire teeming exuberance of life - dead. And all people - dead. **22** Every living, breathing creature that lived on dry land died; **23** he wiped out the whole works - people and animals, crawling creatures and flying birds, every last one of them, gone. Only Noah and his company on the ship lived. **24** The floodwaters took over for 150 days.

## Genesis 8:1-22

**1** Then God turned his attention to Noah and all the wild animals and farm animals with him on the ship. God caused the wind to blow and the floodwaters began to go down. **2** The underground springs were shut off, the windows of Heaven closed and the rain quit. **3** Inch by inch the water lowered. After 150 days the worst was over. **4** On the seventeenth day of the seventh month, the ship landed on the Ararat mountain range. **5** The water kept going down until the tenth month. On the first day of the tenth month the tops of the mountains came into view. **6** After forty days Noah opened the window that he had built into the ship. **7** He sent out a raven; it flew back and forth waiting for the floodwaters to dry up. **8** Then he sent a dove to check on the flood conditions, **9** but it couldn't even find a place to perch - water still covered the Earth. Noah reached out and caught it, brought it back into the ship. **10** He waited seven more days and sent out the dove again. **11** It came back in the evening with a freshly picked olive leaf in its beak. Noah knew that the flood was about finished. **12** He waited another seven days and sent the dove out a third time. This time it didn't come back. **13** In the six-hundred-first year of Noah's life, on the first day of the first month, the flood had dried up. Noah opened the hatch of the ship and saw dry ground. **14** By the twenty-seventh day of the second month, the Earth was completely dry. **15** God spoke to Noah: **16** "Leave the ship, you and your wife and your sons and your sons' wives. **17** And take all the animals with you, the whole menagerie of birds and mammals and crawling creatures, all that brimming prodigality of life, so they can reproduce and flourish on the Earth." **18** Noah disembarked with his sons and wife and his sons' wives. **19** Then all the animals, crawling creatures, birds - every creature on the face of the Earth - left the ship family by family. **20** Noah built an altar to God. He selected clean animals and birds from every species and offered them as burnt-offerings on the altar. **21** God smelled the sweet fragrance and thought to himself, "I'll never again curse the ground because of people. I know they have this bent toward evil from an early age, but I'll never again kill off everything living as I've just done. **22** For as long as Earth lasts, planting and harvest, cold and heat, Summer and winter, day and night will never stop."

**Genesis 9:1-29**
**1** God blessed Noah and his sons: He said, "Prosper! Reproduce! Fill the Earth! **2** Every living creature - birds, animals, fish - will fall under your spell and be afraid of you. You're responsible for them. **3** All living creatures are yours for food; just as I gave you the plants, now I give you everything else. **4** Except for meat with its lifeblood still in it - don't eat that. **5** "But your own lifeblood I will avenge; I will avenge it against both animals and other humans. **6** Whoever sheds human blood, by humans let his blood be shed, Because God made humans in his image reflecting God's very nature. **7** You're here to bear fruit, reproduce, lavish life on the Earth, live bountifully!" **8** Then God spoke to Noah and his sons: **9** "I'm setting up my covenant with you including your children who will come after you, **10** along with everything alive around you - birds, farm animals, wild animals - that came out of the ship with you. **11** I'm setting up my covenant with you that never again will everything living be destroyed by floodwaters; no, never again will a flood destroy the Earth." **12** God continued, "This is the sign of the covenant I am making between me and you and everything living around you and everyone living after you. **13** I'm putting my rainbow in the clouds, a sign of the covenant between me and the Earth. **14** From now on, when I form a cloud over the Earth and the rainbow appears in the cloud, **15** I'll remember my covenant between me and you and everything living, that never again will floodwaters destroy all life. **16** When the

rainbow appears in the cloud, I'll see it and remember the eternal covenant between God and everything living, every last living creature on Earth." **17** And God said, "This is the sign of the covenant that I've set up between me and everything living on the Earth." **18** The sons of Noah who came out of the ship were Shem, Ham, and Japheth. Ham was the father of Canaan. **19** These are the three sons of Noah; from these three the whole Earth was populated. **20** Noah, a farmer, was the first to plant a vineyard. **21** He drank from its wine, got drunk and passed out, naked in his tent. **22** Ham, the father of Canaan, saw that his father was naked and told his two brothers who were outside the tent. **23** Shem and Japheth took a cloak, held it between them from their shoulders, walked backwards and covered their father's nakedness, keeping their faces turned away so they did not see their father's exposed body. **24** When Noah woke up with his hangover, he learned what his youngest son had done. **25** He said, Cursed be Canaan! A slave of slaves, a slave to his brothers! **26** Blessed be God, the God of Shem, but Canaan shall be his slave. **27** God prosper Japheth, living spaciously in the tents of Shem. But Canaan shall be his slave. **28** Noah lived another 350 years following the flood. **29** He lived a total of 950 years. And he died.

# FOREWORD

There are a few people who need to know that when it comes to books, C.E. McAdoo is one of those persons who took hold of education and could not let go. Additionally, Reverend Doctor C. E. McAdoo is a street prognosticator, a seminary sectarian, a denominational dynamo, and a truly gifted human being. Charlie McAdoo could have been on the way to nothingness, but God made an adjustment to the universe. There is simply no earthly explanation for the blessings given to a poor, country boy who had not asked for success but achieved it.

This book may never be on the *New York Times Bestseller* list; yet, the contents will be motivating for many who would venture to read and reflect on the concepts within *Nobody Got Off the Boat*. Here are thoughtful solicitations of someone who has made a life of staying on the boat. Many opportunities were presented to abandon the boat, to disrupt the community, to quit in the crowdedness of the surroundings, but no. This missive presents a life lesson that everyone can use, regardless of age.

The three core foundations of the book, academics, religion, and business, are essentials for prosperous living. Missing one of these foci can lessen the joy we all seek, and God promises, as hopeful and happy people. The book may give the impression of an elementary mission, but don't let that put you in a "trick bag," or a Pandora's box.

You will find that the pages unfold with a reality that penetrates a place you have either been in, you are in, or you are on your way to face. Family, friends, and associates of Dr. McAdoo will enjoy the stories, interpretations, and grassroots dialogue that are brought forth. They all had a choice to live on the boat or die by jumping off. Some folks default to the water. This book will help you see that staying on the boat is the best option.

*Reverend Dr. Vincent Harris*
Houston, Texas 2014

## CHAPTER 1 – BOAT-STAYING PREPARATION
### Before Leaving Shore

If you read the preface, you recall that I referenced the story of Noah and the Ark to share the relationship we have to one another's personal growth and strength. I also offer it to explain this book.

It should be noted first, however, that there is no recording of anyone jumping from the Ark. Simply put, it appears that nobody jumped off the boat. They were all in it together, and they all stayed put.

Why would someone write a book entitled *Nobody Jumped Off the Boat*? Would I buy a book with this title? Writing a book about life as an African American who has been in many settings was a tutorial for me, and many have suggested that I should have jumped off the boat more than once.

For whatever reason, God placed me to be born in a very segregated town, in Lebanon, Tennessee, where African Americans lived in certain communities, and my Caucasian brothers and sisters lived in others. I am a member of the United Methodist Church, which is ninety-five percent white and only five percent African American, and in other arenas that were largely populated by whites, for a great deal of my life. Given my perspective, I think this book will be helpful.

Before southern schools were integrated in the early sixties, I had a little white friend. There were a few whites in the neighborhood I lived in, but it was still at least ninety percent black. At any rate, my little white buddy and I used to play together, and we had a great time. When integration came, he and his family left the neighborhood. This may have been because his family felt uncomfortable living with African Americans. Integration of public schools suggested the beginning of what might spread to everyday life, something not yet experienced in American society. Whites did not go to school with Blacks. I believe that living in close proximity to Blacks and going to school together was just too great an equalizer.

Nonetheless, I grew up in Lebanon and attended Leeman's Corner School, a two-room school for African Americans on the opposite side of town. Our home did not have running water, so we had to tote our own. We had to cut our own firewood, too. All of these things prepared me for life.

Life moved on, and I left Leeman's Corner to go to Market Street Public School when I was ten years old, in the sixth grade. I was sixteen years old when I transferred from Wilson County Public School to Lebanon High School, my first experience with school integration. I was also one of the first of three African Americans to graduate from Lebanon High School. This was in 1965. I graduated from Philander Smith College in Little Rock, Arkansas, a private United Methodist college for African Americans, in 1969. Gloria and I married that August.

I joined the United States Army right after college. I went in with a military platoon that was ninety-five percent white and one hundred percent Arkansan. My bunkmate was from Mountain Top, Arkansas, and had no previous contact with African Americans prior to his induction. Despite what could appear to many as a difficult situation given our nation's history, we really helped one another complete basic training. Fast forward a few more years during my military training and I was a ward master over eighteen people, both black and white. In all these situations in which I found myself, everyone worked together because we were all in it together.

I move now to my thirty-four years in the church, and hope to gain your interest in reading more about nobody jumping off the boat. I was blessed to be appointed to serve as a district superintendent, what some would refer to as a presiding elder or pastoral supervisor, over a number of churches for the southeastern district of the United Methodist Church. I gave the welcome at my first annual meeting as district superintendent in September of 2000 and said, "I'm Black, and you're welcome. And you can't do nothin' about either one of them."

I pray that reading this book will open your eyes to understanding that we are all in life's journey together, and that this is a blessing to us all. I have now touched on some moments, places and situations that I will refer to as boat-staying preparation.  I also want to say that there are no exact formulas to plan where we are going in life, how we can best prepare ourselves, or what boats we must or must not board to end up as we planned.  What I believe, however, is that the base of my boat-staying preparation, my ability to keep from jumping off the boat, was my early home life.

I had two parents who worked every single day, and this really helped me understand the dynamics of responsibility.  My father was not an educated man, and neither was my mother, but both passed on much to me that was of extreme value. I thank my family for preparing me for the journey of life.  I will continue to use the boat analogy because before we get on the boat, we have to prepare ourselves.

My childhood gave me invaluable preparation. It set my values early on. Some folks relate to the two-parent family, and that's how I grew up. Regardless of your family background, however, you must prepare yourself before you get on the boat.

That may sound simplistic, but I really want to home in and talk about particular things that I remember. I'm an old man now, and I probably should have written this book twenty-five years or so ago. I have forgotten much more than I'll ever remember, but I will try to relate the boat-staying preparation I received.

Back in those days, many of us lived in unincorporated areas, and water wasn't provided by cities. My father had to get someone with a backhoe to dig a hole and put a faucet on the other side of my grandmother's house so that we could have water. This faucet attracted others, and many community people would come and use this faucet since they didn't have water at their homes.

My father charged each family twenty-five cents a month for the water they received. I will never forget that there was one family that did not pay the fee. Even so, my father never did stop them from getting water. In terms of how we prepare ourselves to deal with what may happen in life, I believe early preparation in maintaining relationships and how to treat others is critical. I will never know why that family couldn't pay the twenty-five cents a month, and I don't think I need to know. The important thing for me is that my father was able to make sure the water stayed on, and that the family that didn't pay was also able to share in it. That's one notation of a time in life that had a great deal to do with my boat-staying preparation.

The second notation of such a time was when my sister-in-law passed away. After she died, my older brother and his three young children, my nieces and nephew, came to live with us. We lived in a very small house, and I had to move out of my room and sleep on the couch to make room for my brother and his children. The living room became my bedroom, and for those who know about those shotgun houses, there wasn't a whole lot of room at any rate.

We lived through that, and my nieces, nephew and I have an amicable relationship to this day. Although they were little kids and probably did get on my nerves on occasion, that didn't seem to affect me. I say that to say this – I cannot remember an unpleasant moment growing up in that environment, in that house with my family. That's the third notation. My folks did something, maybe they put a psychological screen of some sort over my head, or I missed something that I have yet to recall. That happy childhood prepared me to move forward and to successfully deal with life as I matured.

The fourth notation, one I have to throw in for my grandmother, is the matter of endurance. I'm going to get away from my childhood home in a minute, but must first explain that in the area and time I grew up, the living room could be the same temperature as it was outside. If the temperature was five degrees below freezing at night, the room I lived and slept in was five degrees below freezing as well. There was no central heat or air conditioning, and there was not a stove in my room. This was before the electric blanket, in Lebanon, Tennessee, from my birth in 1948 until 1965.

My grandmother lived right next door. She and my family would put what I believe was a stack of covers about three-feet deep over me on those cold nights. She would also take irons, heat them, and then put them at the base of the bed. I would be able to withstand whatever cold that winter brought with those covers and that heat. I lived there until I left for college. I endured the cold nights as did so many of us because that was our living situation. I got through them and have no negative thoughts about those cold nights. They just prepared me to be in some other uncomfortable places, something else I had to go through as a part of my boat-staying preparation.

So, the base of boat-staying preparation for me was my early childhood. Once we are able to understand what our childhood base gives us, we must look at what else falls within boat-staying preparation, which includes physical preparation. We are in an age where everybody is trying to get in shape or maintain their fitness level. I'm writing this book as an old man who was at one time in much better shape. Before I was able to start my journey as a young person, I had physically prepared myself. This was much easier in those days and in the city where I grew up; we walked everywhere we went. Mine is not the classic story of walking ten miles in the snow to go to school, but I walked everywhere. I was in good shape, too. We did not have to worry about physical education classes because being fit was part of the way we lived. We used to race up and down the street barefooted, and we played all kinds of sports and games.

To be physically prepared to stay on the boat, you have to maintain yourself physically. As this book is being written, I'm getting ready to investigate the Mediterranean diet because I know that I've got to do something about my excess weight. I'm not a huge man, and I don't know if people put this kind of information in their books, but I am five feet and eleven inches tall, and I weigh between two hundred and sixty-two and two hundred and seventy-five pounds. My weight is not where it ought to be. I'm putting this in for boat-staying preparation because staying on the boat has a physical aspect to it. The Lord blessed me to be a preacher for thirty-four years, and I still need physical strength to get up, receive God, and convey God's message. I work out twice a week to maintain good physical strength.

The need for physical strength is in every situation. No matter the job, if we are not physically prepared to take on the daily rigors of it and go from one place to another as needed, we are not helping ourselves. Without physical strength, we will not be able to stay on the boat to do what we are to do. We need a healthy diet and a diet plan, but we need to have something that we will follow. I am working on my diet plan and will start with what I like, which can sometimes set in motion a personal challenge.

I like fatback, a type of pig fat. I recently went into a restaurant and ordered some roast beef. I told the lady to cut a little fatback and put it on my meat. I like salt in my food, too. These are two of the things I've got to change to be successful. I mention this challenge in this physical preparation piece to say that I can't continue to eat the way I have been and expect to have strength and stamina. Two of my young grandsons came to town this past weekend, and I wasn't really able to play with them because I was not physically prepared.

As we continue with the Noah story as our base, know that there will be more about that forty-day phenomenon of his time on the Ark throughout this book. When preparing to go anywhere for over a month, we need to be physically prepared. Our first boat-staying preparation is with our family base and what we learned there, and the second is having a good understanding of physical capacity and condition. The third thing we need to talk about in our boat-staying preparation is that we must be mentally prepared.

I am not a psychologist or psychiatrist, but I was blessed to have had training in the military as a psychiatric technician with certification in psychiatric procedures. Because I likely know only enough to be dangerous when it comes to the mental aspects of life, I will focus on anecdotes about being mentally prepared for staying on the boat and all of us being together there.

Getting mentally prepared means realizing that our egos are more fragile than we anticipate. I remember some of the training I received in the military. The psychiatrists I worked with talked about life as something we all lived on what they referred to as "the line," and that we try to stay in a mental condition that keeps us as close to that line as possible. The same psychiatrists said that when we get too high over the line or too far beneath it, emotional problems can result. I believe that to prepare to stay on the boat, we have to mentally prepare to stay close to that line. Part of that mental preparation lets us know that when we are dealing with people with different views from our own, they may rub us the wrong way. Even when we are dealing with people with whom we are very close, if we do not stay close to that line, we can easily go too high over it, or too low under it, very quickly. Mood swings, or movement too far from the line that we discussed earlier, do not prepare us to stay on the boat long.

Think about it. We find no story of anyone jumping off the boat, but I wonder if Noah and his crew had to throw somebody off the boat, or at least wished that they could. We can be in such an emotional state that people just don't want to be around us. So let me again reference this in terms of boat-staying preparation. We have to be emotionally ready to deal with whatever may come. I won't get into the particular psychological aspects of how one might do this but I will say we need to maintain - and this is folk psychology again – some distance.

To be prepared emotionally, we need to have some distance from whatever we are dealing with to succeed. I am not talking about using drugs other than those prescribed by a physician, or any other kind of foreign substance, but just the ability to mentally remove oneself. During the Vietnam War from 1969 to 1971, I was a psychiatric technician and served as a psychiatric ward master. I did not have to go on the trips that the other corpsmen did. They took men to occupational therapy and did other activities with them, and I stayed on the ward. I began to get anxious being on the ward, so I discussed my feelings with the psychiatrist who said, "What you need to do, McAdoo, is get away from the ward sometimes." So, what I started doing each day, unbeknownst to my wife or anyone else, was to get in my vehicle and drive around the post. Sometimes I would make a full circle around the base, or I would drive to certain areas and just sit and meditate, and then I was mentally prepared to go back to the ward.

I will never forget one patient on the psychiatric ward who was acting out so that we had to walk him to the "quiet room," a padded room away from the other patients.

As we walked him down the corridor and approached an area with a door with four panes of glass at the top, this patient got into a karate stance, and kee-yah! He broke that glass with a straight punch and continued walking. We gently continued the walk to our destination. Hear me when I say that the man probably had a black belt in karate or some other martial art. He broke the glass, suffered no cuts, and never said a word! I don't know what was going on in his mind, but regardless of where I had been that day or whatever frame of mind I had gotten up in that morning, I was emotionally prepared to remain silent, and I did. I was not by myself on this walk down the corridor. I was with another corpsman, and we were with the man who broke the glass. We walked on as if nothing happened, and the patient entered the quiet room. I don't know what he did next because we didn't film patients in their rooms in those days. But the key, once again, is that in order to be on life's boat, we have to be mentally prepared. Number one in that regard is to maintain some distance.

The second part of mental preparation is active honesty. Active honesty is what we have to do with ourselves about situations in life that affect us emotionally and cause us to want to be less than honest with ourselves and others.

We all have these moments. Many of us are so private that we just don't want to let folks know how vulnerable we are to those feelings and the stress that can result. We must be honest in our relationships with others, with our spouse or significant other, our children, friends and family, and people at work. We have to be honest professionally, in how we relate to others in various ranks of authority and status. Active honesty is the second place that prepares us to stay on the boat. Maintaining both our distance and our core beliefs helps to prepare us emotionally to deal with difficult situations.

The third thing I want to talk about in terms of being emotionally prepared is joyful affirmation. I tell you, there is nothing better than being around someone full of joy! It almost shows through us when we stay on the positive side and avoid the negative. Joyful affirmation means to keep in mind that we are blessed to be alive. That sounds so simple, doesn't it?

Joyful affirmation is sometimes more of a mental break, not a mental block, but a mental breakthrough. If we have the breakthrough of joyful affirmation, we can better manage our emotions in relation to what is going on that day. And remember that if we are thinking about staying on the boat, we must be emotionally prepared.

Lastly, we must be spiritually prepared for boat-staying preparation. This speaks to our relationship to God or a higher power. To stay on the boat and know that we are all in this together, we have to be spiritually prepared to deal with others. We relate to that spirituality in different ways. I believe that we are all blessed by God in every aspect of our lives, and that we are blessed by His presence whether or not we are Christian. As a United Methodist, I affirm that, and I believe in the whole Bible. And there are things in the Bible that give me a headache, too! There are such joys, hopes, love, and victory, but there are also rapes, murder, and backstabbing. The Bible is often heavy reading, indeed.

So, to be spiritually prepared to stay on the boat, we need a spiritual base that covers it all. That means for me that sometimes we are going to be up and sometimes we are going to be down, depending on what is going on in our lives. Some situations are so overwhelming to us that without a spiritual base, we would find ourselves unable to overcome them. That's the key to being spiritually prepared to stay on the boat – to know that we are going to run into obstacles that will require an ability to overcome. The Scriptures say it a little better with the message that there are evils in high places.

There is another force in the world that is out there to move us from our spiritual base. We all face trials and tribulations. The Scripture says the sun and the rain come on the good and the bad, meaning they fall on us all. So, to be spiritually prepared to stay on the boat and know that we are all in this together, we know that when one of us is having a bad day, another is having a good day. Thus, when people are up, they can help another who is down. For Christians, that means that we are a people who have a base in Jesus, our Lord and Savior, and through the Holy Spirit that dwells within us. It always amused me when I was growing up that we had young men who would often use God's name in vain, but as soon as they went up for a rebound on the basketball court and hurt themselves, the first thing they would say was "Oh Lord, help me." It turns out we all have a need to believe in something greater than ourselves at some point.

I believe that with a good family base, physical fitness, a balanced emotional life, and our spirituality, we will be able to get on the boat and be well prepared to remain.

## CHAPTER 2 – LIVING AND THRIVING IN THE LAND OF OPPOSITION
### Choppy Waters

I begin this chapter by pointing out that no one knows the progression of the families or animals as they boarded the Ark. Many of us can visualize the classic scene of them entering the Ark two-by-two, however. Just think of the first two that entered. What must it have been like? We can think of it figuratively or literally, but the story is about a lesson, a life lesson. We can't say which animals went in first, but we can imagine them boarding. Think of the first few animals that went in and watched the rest continue to board. Let's say one group of animals boarded and shortly after watched another group board, one with whom they were dire enemies. The essence of this chapter, Living and Thriving in the Land of Opposition, is that of survival. So let me flip that scenario from the animal kingdom to the human world as we study living and thriving with others.

We're all in this together, so what do we do when we find ourselves in that land of opposition? And what does that mean? Sometimes, being in that land is a result of who we are. If you are a male, you will be in situations where there are more females. It follows that if you are a female, you will find yourself in places where there are more males. If you are Black you will find yourself in situations where there are more whites, or more Hispanics . . . the list goes on and on. We also find ourselves in situations in which we are in the minority or majority educationally or socially. At the root of our success in the land of opposition is the ability to ask ourselves how to best live and even thrive.

To live is to understand that life is a journey, and so we must understand the importance and value of life's journey at its best. If we look at life as having the highest premium or value, we understand that life is not punctuated with periods. I believe we live within a series of commas until the end comes, or the period. To live our fullest is to understand the need to change. It is so easy to talk about change and about the opportunity that living gives us to affect that change. We live lives that consist of much more than just eating and sleeping; the remainder of our days is spent living those other moments. As long as we are alive, we have the ability to make contact with others, another blessing God has given us.

The nature of contact leads to communication, and that leads to understanding. The nature of understanding leads to knowing that we are all in this together. We should get up every day of our lives with a plan of what we wish to do that day. And we want to make sure we communicate with the world around us in order to do the things we wish that require the support of others. Understanding is established through our interaction with others, and we increase that understanding throughout our lives. This is the relational aspect of living.

Although we share in communication and understanding, we all live our lives within unique situations. I am blessed to have pastored in the largest gated community in Arkansas, in Hot Springs Village. And I understand real estate exclusion, meaning that I know that not everyone can enter Hot Springs Village at free will. I recall that residents had a card to permit their entrance into the community, and there were security guards at each side of the gate. I crossed countless times between that closed community and a more open type of living. I also knew, as did others who lived in that community, that there were others who lived a life way that suggested they knew that there was life outside those gates, and good people, too. There are many who prefer a more closed community, and that is all right; we are free in this country to live our lives as we please. While living in our communities of choice, however, it is important to communicate within and outside our chosen community. Living with an openness to those from within and outside allows us further understanding and contact, both of which allow us to thrive.

As a child of the Sixties, I witnessed a great deal of change in American society. I was an eighteen- year-old in 1965, when the Voter Rights Act was passed. This information may be difficult to recall or even learn about for some, so I will share it. In the past, many American states demanded that African Americans pass what were referred to as "literacy tests" before being allowed to vote. The questions given were meant to be unanswerable, without a previously determined answer. Questions such as how many bubbles are in a bar of Dial soap come to mind. It may be difficult to believe, but this sort of harassment was used to keep Blacks from voting, and it occurred on both sides of the Mason-Dixon line, both "down south" and "up south." Living in the northern part of this country did not mean that African Americans were spared the opposition of the blatant discrimination of the times.

I believe that American society has moved away, to some extent, from racism to classism. Classism may be the biggest barrier today, although ageism, sexism, and all those other isms are still with us. We also have discrimination against those with disabilities, those who are homosexual, those who are non-Christian, and others I may have missed. Almost any difference from the majority creates an opposite, one who is different and in the minority. Once that occurs, isms tend to follow. We all move within and between different environments and experience isms, some of us much more so than others.

How do we move from just living to thriving in such opposition? I have a four-step process that I think will help us, a tiered process. First, we start noting what is happening in our lives. A daily journal is fine but not necessary. Key words entered that describe each day are useful. I hope that as you make daily entries and examine the words over given periods of time that you notice you have entered reflection statements as well as single words. Another way to accomplish this may be when you come home and talk with your significant other or additional household members. If this isn't possible, consider conversations you have on a daily basis as a place to notice what occurs, and record that. Keep a record of these conversations and the anecdotes that often result.

I was blessed to work for the United States Postal Service in 1977. One of my buddies there, Tom Banks, who is now ninety-six years old, suggested that I keep a list of everything that happened each work day. When I asked him why, he said, "Well, you know they, management, are writing stuff down about you every single day. You need to write something down about them, too."

During my time at the post office, I was part of two law suits concerning illegal management practices. When I left each evening, my supervisor had often already punched our time cards to "clock us out" for the day, which impacted how much we were paid. I did not think anything about it at the time, nor did I write anything down. The result of one law suit was clarity regarding the use of time cards to indicate employee arrival to, and departure from, the workplace. As one would expect, it was determined that employees, not management, were to use employee time cards to indicate their status during work hours.

The second suit had to do with gross inequities when it came to the possibility of promotion of Blacks to management positions. Whenever a black employee was to be considered for a supervisory position, the qualifications became very fluid. This allowed for a type of discrimination that was, supposedly, based on who was best qualified. If a college degree was required, for example, a position would be listed with a given number of years of experience or "technical efficiency," another arbitrary term, that could serve to make sure an otherwise qualified minority candidate was excluded. This situation was also settled in court. You should remember that this was before African Americans, women and other minorities were considered worthy of promotion or even serious consideration of it. Only years of intervention have resulted in change in this regard.

So, like many others at one time or another, I was living in the land of opposition at my work place. A number one priority for striving, then, is to have some way of noting, whether in a journal or electronically, things that happen in daily life. Think how relaxing it might be to come in and write your notes of the day. For most of us, it would be helpful if we had that much discipline. Even notes made weekly or monthly might be of use. Whether they are work related or not, keeping notes can enable you thrive in the land of opposition, wherever you may find yourself in the minority.

When you are striving in the land of opposition, remember that you have already made the decision to live. Once you have made this decision, you must be ready to thrive, the second stance for striving. To do so, you need to find out what is really working and what cannot work, and you have to recognize both. Each of us is unique, but we are all in situations in which we are able to see what works best to thrive where we are. All of us are in situations where we find out what works. If you get nothing else out of this book, I hope you will remember that no one has absolute expertise on living and thriving. No one has been precisely where you have been, within the communities in which you have lived, and with the particular emotions you have experienced.

My children would tell you that I am a proponent of Einstein's Theory of Relativity; they mention it frequently as they've heard it from me so often. I have told them many, many times that they have to understand that we cannot precisely re-create what has already occurred, which is why life is a relative journey. Any scientist can tell you that they cannot precisely replicate something that has happened before. They can run the same experiment each day, but the results will differ, if only slightly. The relative humidity could be different, or the person conducting the experiment could change. There will always be slight differences that affect each result.

But in the midst of our determination to live, we do learn that there are some things that work well for us. Once we find out what does work in a given situation, we should focus on that. Second, we should ask ourselves how we can improve on what works, because we are all in this together, within this land of opposites. If we are to live here together, we need to find ways to improve our lives within a community.

Consider commerce. If you are in a business and your business makes no profit, you are alive but your profit baseline is zero. Your business won't continue at zero for long. If someone says, "Wow, let's see if we can improve on this and move from zero to one," you may move from zero to one. If that works, you have begun to make progress, and at some point, profit.

When I was in college, I worked in the summer for the Sherwin-Williams Paint Company. I made paint. On my first day, this white man, another employee of the company, came up to me and said "By God, you know I don't like niggers." I said to him, "Well, I don't eat them either." He became one of my best work friends because I knew where he stood. Of course, I still tried to help him at work, and he helped me understand the union work environment as well as many work-related tasks. I share the story of this man and our working relationship within my

18

chapter about thriving in the land of opposition because it proves a point. You might ask, "Now, when that man said that to you, why didn't you smack him upside the head?" Look, I was a college student and I was trying to do my work and keep my job. I felt I cut back to him as hard as I could, and I did. We got along for three years, and I kept that job in Chicago, Illinois, at Sherwin-Williams Paint Company because I had built a strong relationship with that man, and with my supervisor.

Later, my supervisor did something that helped me along even further in terms of understanding my situation and where I wanted to land. He wanted what was best for the company, something I learned about him during my second summer there. I had a chance to work with an anti-poverty program on weekdays that summer, and my supervisor developed a job on the night shift that allowed me to work with the anti-poverty program and stay with the paint company. He told me that he assigned me the work that others on the night shift wouldn't get done. My supervisor knew that what was best for the company could also be best for an employee.

As I mentioned previously, in business you can move from zero to one, from one to two, from two to three, and improve business and the profit generated. We ask questions in hopes that people can come together to improve a product or service, and to increase the profit that results. We look at ways to improve processes and products. We can do this in the land of opposition when we focus on what we are trying to achieve as a group rather than on our own difference or that of others. This is good for business and employees.

Our third level of striving is to share a common, well-established goal. Regardless of the enterprise, once a common goal is set for a person or group, there should be an understanding that leads us to strive for something that each of us can do to help achieve that goal. We may wish to increase profits, to build a better building or manufacture

19

a better product. Once we get a goal that is common to everyone, there are a couple of ways to go. First of all, in good striving we can set a point at which we will begin movement toward our goal. Second, we should have an end point at which we are done, or at least a midway or set of points at which we should take measure. I prefer to use increments of three months, and to review progress toward a goal within three-month stages. If a goal isn't accomplished within about eighteen months it bears either serious re-tooling or the need to move on to something else. The positive aspect of this model of goal setting is that we thrive within a group that works together, even if the goal isn't met.

In addition to living, thriving, and approaching a common goal within increments of time, the third thing we should do is to commit ourselves to learning as much as we can about our product or what we are trying to achieve. Contributing knowledge toward the goal to be achieved is a powerful thing, and can result in better circumstances even when forces outside impact the end result.

When I was pastoring the Hot Springs Village United Methodist Church, I was prepared when it came to the difficulties of the 2008 recession. I researched what chief executive officers were doing in terms of salary adjustments during the recession, and worked with my executive staff to put together a salary modification that enabled a staff of thirteen to be somewhat happy with the result. Pressures and politics often occur in such matters, but progress and thriving together can still produce results. All situations, church, school, or work, challenge us. Yet, the goal can be achieved.

Difficult times call for fairness and concern for all, the fourth level of striving. The "across the board" concept frequently comes up in situations in which limited resources are involved. Salary cuts work as long as we understand the impact of cutting the same percentage on everyone. There is a real difference that cut makes to

20

someone paid ten thousand dollars a year or less as compared to someone else making one hundred thousand dollars or more. People with lower salaries are impacted much more negatively by those cuts than those who make much more. Learning from outside resources enables us to approach thriving with greater creativity, flexibility, and fairness in a variety of situations.

Approaching situations with as much education and information as possible allows for the sharing of needed facts and honoring that we are all in this together. I also think that information helps us to stop going in circles! Living and thriving mean that we must move forward. The idea of writing this book came to me around the time I decided I was going to retire. It lay dormant for a while, but after all, I had those thirty-two years in ministry. I had been a supervisory pastor for eight of those years, as well as a consultant. I felt this book would be something that could help other people and me, too.

I think everyone should write a book. This is my third, part of a collection I named "The Journey Series." My children have written books as well; we have several books written within the family at this point. As difficult as it is at times, we must realize that if we want to do anything, we've got to just do it. It can be very frustrating to get started, and writing is often a slow process. Once we stop circling around the task of writing, however, we can discover story lines and positive aspects of life. We can also learn about people, including ourselves, who are in the land of opposition at one time or another, and how that impacts them.

The fifth way we strive and thrive in that land of opposition is to have personal affirmation. I remember a time when I was leaving Arkansas to return to Kansas City, Missouri, to seminary school. I had stopped at a service station in northern Arkansas. I drove up to the pump, got out, and discovered that the service station worker had not turned on the pump when I drove up. Thinking he had not seen me, I went into the station and no one there said a word to me, not one word. I decided that I had been seen, so I went back out expecting to pump my gas, pay and leave. But they still hadn't turned on the pump.

Thinking that I was born at night but not last night, I drove to the next service station, an Exxon. I always carried an Exxon card back then. The man at the Exxon station treated me exactly as that bunch had at the first station. I was standing there unable to pump gas until I began to explain that I had sense enough to know that Exxon's headquarters was located in Houston, Texas, and that I was ready to call there and tell them that I was unable to buy gas at this Exxon location. I was absolutely furious at that point, and I am sure I was quite loud. I finally got my gas though. Then I headed straight back to Kansas City. I never drove that particular highway again, and when I think about it, I get that headache I mentioned in Chapter One, the one that comes when I read of scandalous events in the Bible.

I want to emphasize the need for personal affirmation. When I was trying to fill my gas tank, I was not going to let anyone take away my personal affirmation, my dignity, or my pride. I think when we are striving in the land of opposition, we have to stop and take our personal affirmation seriously, very seriously, indeed.

So, remember we can strive when we write it down; decide to live; set a goal; be fair and concerned; and have personal affirmation. While these waters may be choppy, we must still sail.

## CHAPTER 3 – UNDERSTANDING A STANCE OF STEADINESS
**Steady as She Goes**

You know, today's need for instant gratification does not allow steadiness to maintain the kind of stature that it once had. When I was growing up, we admired folks that were steady. I believe that nobody jumped off the boat, Noah's Ark, because they were all in this together. In order to stay together, then and now, it stands to reason that everyone on the boat has to have a sense of steadiness. This isn't always a visual characteristic. It may not be something easily articulated, but a stance of steadiness was necessary then, and remains so today.

Again, I will use the story of Noah and the Ark to illustrate. Those on the Ark had no knowledge of how long they would remain there. They only knew it would rain until God determined that the rain would end. Imagine what could have occurred if there had been no stance of steadiness within those aboard. They knew that rain would come; there was no question about that. The only question was when. And when the rain did come, the folks on the Ark did not know how long it would last. What they had to do was to become steady. With steadiness comes wisdom, an ability to grasp why steadiness is necessary. Steadiness also enables us to move to the relational aspect of what we are trying to do. We hold on, and we begin to understand.

Those on the Ark were like us, living everyday lives and developing the understanding that helps maintain a stance of steadiness. What this means and how we think of it works in all aspects of life, in any setting where people interact. I am writing with religion, business and education in mind, although this concept certainly extends beyond those three. There is a certain part of boat-staying that has to do with steadiness for a number of reasons. Sometimes the boat itself can be unsteady because of choppy waters. Just because the boat is unsteady doesn't mean we have to be unsteady, however.

Let us talk now about understanding and developing our stance of steadiness in relation to the environments we find ourselves in. While a neighborhood may be unsteady, that doesn't mean we have to be. The same holds true for classrooms, churches, or work. Just because the church you are in is unsteady doesn't mean you have to be. Even if the management team or the supervisor you work with is unsteady, you can retain your stance. In order for us to move on and remain on the boat, we must remember that we are all in this together, and we've got to be steady. You may ask, "Well, if I'm steady, what about those folks who aren't?" This is where the magnetic effect takes place. It only takes one to maintain steadiness, and steadiness tends to attract others. For the most part, if two people are positive and steady, others will likely join them.

We can't worry about all the unsteadiness around us. What we need to focus on is finding that person, that partner to help us maintain our steadiness. This further develops our relationships and our own steadiness stance.

Find someone around you that has a similar mindset about your goals and aspirations, and remember that they don't have to think the same as you.

I've been blessed to have had a good friend, Ivria Johnson, Jr., for many years, from the time we were college roommates in 1966 until his death in 2015. We bounced ideas off one another every day, and that helped us maintain our stance of steadiness. Like many people, I think I am right ninety-six percent of the time. I ran something by this good friend once, confident that he would affirm me. Instead, he said, "Oh no, Mac. Uh, I think that is ...well, this might not be..." Instead of affirming my every thought, he offered me another perspective that was more than worthy of my consideration. I still maintain that steadiness through his memory.

I am aware that this type of relationship, this opportunity to remain steady through close interaction with others, can be difficult at times. Most of us don't appreciate being told that we are wrong. We don't want anybody to critique our ideas, but considering that critique is the first step to further developing our stance of steadiness. Our steadiness continues to develop when we interact with those who really understand who we are and how we make decisions. Developing these relationships is the first step toward improving our steadiness.

If there's nothing else for which I thank the church from my years of experience there, it would be that I had a bishop, a leader, who helped me maintain my steadiness. Our bishop sent us to several training sessions about personality differences, something I think of even today. It worried me that she was always sending those of us she led for so much training. I now realize that what she was actually doing resulted in her learning more about us.

I'll use the color scheme assessment, for example, as one model used in training we received. How we responded to a question or scenario would result in whether we were labeled a particular color. Some would be in the yellow group while others would be in the blue group or some other color. I learned that our bishop did not want to have teams made up of just one color or people who, based on personality traits, always thought the same way. You can critique these personality tests forever, of course, and many do. It could be the case that not everyone involved in designing these experiences is a professional. But I now understand that the bishop wanted us to see that we needed to work with people who didn't always see things the way we did. We need people who have different perspectives from ours. The second step of developing steadiness is to find somebody who will tell the truth, even if we don't want to hear it.

When we came to Philander Smith College in 1965, the Scripture we first heard was John 8:32, "You shall know the truth and the truth shall set you free." The other thing about knowing the truth was how the grading scale worked at Philander Smith College. We learned that no grades of D would be put on our transcripts. We would work until we achieved A's, B's or C's, period. The school expected every student to be at least average, if not better. So, you shall know the truth and the truth shall set you free at Philander Smith College meant that we could not be graduates of the college unless we had at least a C average. We knew that D's did not count toward graduation. Therefore, part of my steadiness in college was that I knew I had to make a C or better in every course.

We have to move forward to continue to refine this sense of steadiness. When we go to school or our jobs, to our religious institutions or back to our own communities, there is always some level of unsteadiness. Some places may appear to have little steadiness, say twenty percent, and maybe we can deal with that. If the sense of steadiness grows, our sense of steadiness grows within that place, too. Some of us require a greater sense of steadiness than others, but each of us requires some sense of steadiness within ourselves and others, and that sense impacts our interaction in every place we find ourselves.

I want to mention a few more strategies that can help us to work our way through our days and improve our own personal stance of steadiness, one of which is to develop a daily routine. I have a certain routine that starts from getting up each morning to walking out the door. I choose a morning prayer and meditation time to thank God for blessing me and getting me through the night. Others may choose to reflect, to think of people and situations for which they are grateful. This doesn't have to take a great deal of time. Fifteen seconds or up to two or three minutes per day would do because most of us just jump up and start the day. Everyone's routine is going to be a bit different, however.

I also suggest some kind of meditation. Meditation and conversation with others, along with attending to your personal hygiene, are good ways to start the day. They are also invigorating. You may recall that I mentioned diet in the first chapter of this book. Whatever your dietary routine is, you want to think about that and be mindful of it throughout your day. Some folks exercise in the morning, and others start the day with their newspaper. For those folks, exercise comes later. The important thing is to have a daily routine.

Third, as you are moving through your day, try to keep a pleasant thought and understanding of what that means, including acknowledgement of those around you. If you are in a household with someone, this acknowledgement should include speaking to all in your home. If that isn't part of your habit, I suggest you incorporate it because it is just a good thing. If you have slept in bed with somebody that night, do you not speak to them the next morning? If you have children, do you not speak to them in the morning? You may have other relatives living with you, and you should speak to them as well.

Remember, nobody but you can see to it that you are pleasant and thoughtful! As you begin your commute, day at work, school or church, a routine helps. I have commuted as much as two hours a day sometimes, and I had one commute that took as little as seven minutes. When commuting from my home to my job, I try to have good and pleasant thoughts. I want to arrive and not have to say a word to anyone about how I am feeling that day. I would hope and pray that others will see within me that we are all in this together. I also want them to see that I am certainly not ready to jump off the boat. I think this helps in building a sense of steadiness.

My oldest son - and I will interject my children and grandchildren throughout this book - helped me come up with a concept. Many years ago, he and I came to an understanding that we've got more money than we've got time, and that should not throw time away. Going back once again to Einstein's Theory, we're not going to get back those minutes that have passed. They cannot be recreated. Time will never return, so we should covet every minute we have in life. When we understand that, our time becomes more precious to us. We should also understand the financial aspect of time and make sure that we don't give our time away at work. We should work and do the very best at whatever we do, and we should get paid for it. Our time is valuable. I am retired, and my time is valuable still, whether I am consulting or not. When we work, we are paid for our time. It shouldn't be taken from us without consideration.

You have now likely guessed that the fourth aspect of steadiness is an awareness of the value of time. It has taken time to put this book together, and I value this time. Learning to value time is a very good habit. I have a paper calendar, and I write appointments and things I need to attend to on it. I have developed this routine of valuing time that helps others value my time, too. Meetings are just one place where time can slip away from us. If I serve as a committee chair, for example, I see to it that each meeting starts and ends on time. If the meeting is to start at 6:00 pm, I have a time alert announced at 6:55 pm. That means we are going to stop the meeting at 7:00 pm. In my opinion, if we can't do our business in an hour as planned then some of us, myself included, have probably been talking too much, or we need to extend out time for that one meeting.

We also deal with unsteadiness around us during times of turmoil. Readers may recall that in the past several years, vacation cruise lines have had problems with stranded ships. In the midst of the chaos and unsteadiness that happened with one ship in 2013, conditions were horrible. People became sick, the climate was miserable, and fresh food and drinking water were unavailable for several days. It should be noted that nobody jumped off the boat, however, even though it was full of unsteady people in an unsteady situation. Those aboard made their way, and they lived through it.

Another positive aspect of valuing our time enables us to transfer that value to someone. In other words, when we say we give our time to a person, a project or cause, we may be doing public service or special projects that require significant hours of work beyond our normal work schedule.

Valuing our time adds to the steadiness we are trying to achieve in our personal lives. Earlier in this chapter, I talked about personal ways to steady yourself with the establishment a daily routine. Once again, I'll pull from my own experiences. I was an old man when I decided to go back to school for graduate education in seminary, and when I went back I found out I couldn't write well. I had been away from my Philander Smith college undergraduate days for about fifteen years, and I hadn't written a sentence since then, much less a paper. I even took remedial reading. I don't think the school knew I was doing that. I just knew I wasn't doing well in class, and I knew what I had to do to improve.

After I submitted my first paper in seminary, I went home and told my wife, "Well, you know, they will probably promote me on up to the next level, and I won't have to stay up here in this seminary but about a year. They are really going to pass me on." I got my paper back and it looked like the Red Sea! The professor had written all over it. Evidently, what I was thinking had not always made it to the page, and I had made many errors in grammar and punctuation. I was not prepared to write a full sentence, and the professor noted that there were gaps in my writing, with words and phrases missing. It was quite embarrassing. Here I was, an older man who had quit his job, a good job, who had also left his home and gone off to seminary, and I couldn't even write a sentence. The reading class also prepared us for speedreading. Part of the speed reading technique also helped us with taking exams, and it was a physical exercise. I was taught to touch both sides of my head at the temples, the pulse points, as a way to relax and focus. Even now, when I am preparing to do something and need to find steadiness, I can sit in a chair, locate those pulse points at my temples, and relax. I am glad that I learned this technique, and I like what it does for me. There are many meditative techniques available, and I believe that we all can benefit from learning those that work best for us, particularly in times where we might panic a bit. Working our way through those times of anxiety helps to maintain the stance for steadiness. It makes for sailing that is referred to as "steady as she goes," regardless of the choppy waters we sometimes must navigate.

## CHAPTER 4 – SELF-GIVING
### Bon Voyage

The boat sailed, the rain came, and you were prepared. You have lived in the world of opposition, and now you are steady. There is another depth to the steadiness that I want to talk about now. It has to do with how we are staying on the boat, and why we are all in this together. I want to talk about selflessness, the giving of oneself for the good of others. I think selflessness is very freeing, and it makes our lives worth living.

After I wrote my master's thesis, I developed it into a book entitled *Soul Prints of Faith*. I dealt with sin in the book, and how sin imprisons us. Our selfishness imprisons us as well. It's so easy to be selfish, to be self-centered. I find myself still being prayerful and apologetic when I go to God. Some things that might seem minute to others still bother me because of my desire to always be right, which is selfish.

In order to give of ourselves, we have to free ourselves from the jail of selfishness, which can lead to a sinful perspective. As we reflect on the Ark, I feel it safe to say that every man, woman, and animal aboard most likely wanted things done a certain way. I usually find that to be the case no matter where I am. In school, at work, at church, and in our communities, everyone wants things done to his or her own liking. I believe the selfishness that drives this desire is present in every part of our lives, regardless of our actual location at the moment.

For example, I'm always amazed at the hypocrisy of our governmental systems. I recently saw on the news that one of the largest banks in America lost an enormous amount of money. This loss happened at the expense of others. This is commonly known as greed, and in this case, theft. The need to have our way cannot override the understanding that we are all in this together. That's one thing that did not happen in the Noah story. People on the Ark did have some understanding of self and how to free themselves from selfishness. This is one of the hardest things in the world to do. I may not have all the answers, but I do know we must talk about selfishness honestly.

I talked earlier about that partner that we need to bounce things off, someone who knows us, but we must start with what I call soul mining. You don't mine your soul with a spade or a big shovel, either. You mine your soul with a Caterpillar backhoe, meaning something that digs deep. No one can do that deep digging for us, either. Each of us has to do that deep soul mining for ourselves. As I said earlier, this book is part of a journey series. This is the kind of book that you read for yourself so that you might understand the whole concept of self and self-giving.

On today's television reality shows, on the radio and the internet, everyone has information to share about how we should look into ourselves and seek individual freedom. It appears to me that media personalities are often encouraging people to say and do whatever they want to, to be quite selfish and self-centered. Very small children often behave this way because they are in their natural state; they have yet to learn better. Fortunately, maturity cures many ills. As a matter of fact, research now indicates that the frontal lobe of the brain does not fully develop until we are about twenty-five years old.

If we are all in this together and are to be free, we must first know ourselves. For example, consider imprisonment. If you were actually in jail, you could get a lawyer to develop a defense, and a court date would be assigned; there is a process to be followed to attempt to be freed from jail. I can't offer a process for how to achieve selflessness and personal freedom, however. This process comes more from within.

This will differ for each of us, but I will begin with the assumption that you are not incarcerated. Although a prison sentence can end, we are never truly free from that which has been attached to us since we were small children. Things we don't know about or recall still affect our lives. Nevertheless, we must free ourselves of self-centeredness as much as possible before we can give freely of ourselves. Then, we must still remain vigilant and guard against a return to a self-centered state.

It may appear that those we have learned about through our study of history have freed themselves, at least to a certain point. We should remember, however, that the only person to fully free himself and give of himself one hundred percent was Jesus. Others may feel the same about certain prophets they believe achieved such a selfless state. I look at Gandhi as an individual who was significant in our history. He sought to free himself from selfishness so that he could give freely of himself to others.

I don't know if this is necessarily something that can be achieved quickly in church, in school or at work. I do know that supervisors, in order to help the company to be more productive, have to free themselves when they talk with co-workers. Then, an understanding develops about being in this together and trying to make a better product, increase profit or provide better service. In church, for example, people are not going to be easily freed from selfishness if they are used to having things done their own way. People can be shown this freedom by others. It can also be transferred to them, however, through God's work and the power of His ministry.

We must free ourselves so that we can give to others without our egos, our jealousies, and our misunderstandings getting in the way. We must also understand that as humans, we will never reach perfection but must continue to monitor our selfishness to become truly giving of ourselves. Once again, how to accomplish this falls to each of us. We need to look in the mirror at ourselves, and be careful not to see ourselves through the eyes of others. We know ourselves best.

I wouldn't begin to suggest when or how often this mirror date might occur, but we do need to look at ourselves regularly with an eye toward what we wish to achieve. We should ask ourselves who we are, and then define the essence of what we wish to contribute. We need to ask what it is that we hope to accomplish and who we want to be, and we need to stay in front of that mirror until we have the data we are there to collect. The answers we get help us form the selfless model.

This selfless profiling is not easy, particularly for many of us who have been in settings where we have been the only one, the minority in that land of opposition, at work, church, or school. When we wake up in the morning, look in the mirror, and think we look nothing like the people we will be dealing with that day, we contribute to a mindset of anxiety. We would be better off reflecting on what we are trying to accomplish instead of thinking about potential obstacles.

When we take that last look in the mirror each morning after dressing, or when we come home in the evening, are we looking in the mirror and asking ourselves who we are or how things went that day? Similar to the journaling or taking notes that I discussed in an earlier chapter, this is when we can take a moment and realize that we are glad to be on the boat with others in our lives, and that we are not thinking of jumping off. We can also realize the personal gratitude that comes from the realization that we are not on the boat alone. This approach also helps us to be positive about ourselves.

After you go through the process above, I think you will be in a much better position to understand the concept of prolonged enduring, something that comes from both inside and outside ourselves. Prolonged enduring has a lot to do with where we've been, but it also shapes who we continue to be. It says a lot about our self-giving, too. Some information from my seminary school experience may help here.

Many people judge the human condition with perfection in mind, and find themselves disappointed when others fall below this impossible standard. They ask why a person would fail, or how such behavior could occur. Over thirty years ago in seminary training, I learned about the systemic nature of life. We were taught to start from the bottom, or total depravity, when considering the human condition. We were taught to help ourselves and others move to a state of increased selflessness. Speaking from the theological perspective then, I'm never totally shocked by anything that humans do. People are capable of doing deplorable things, and as I said earlier about what we find in the Bible, we know that sometimes people have caused others to suffer prolonged enduring.

I will talk about the human condition from the perspective of an African American and the prolonged enduring that results from that experience. When you think about the history of African Americans in the United States, you realize that African royalty and others went from freedom in their homeland to slavery in America. Then, we went from some semblance of freedom through the segregation of Jim Crow laws to the beginnings of the struggle for civil rights and integration. Today, it is clear that prolonged enduring is the result.

African Americans will continue to endure the remnants of the history of slavery and racism that are still with us today. We understand that what occurred is against our nature. It is incomprehensible that African Americans were once enslaved and now bear the prolonged enduring of it, the continuing effects of that history. A sense of both self and self-giving is part of prolonged enduring, as is the knowledge that whites share that history as well. Neither race has the ability to erase what happened, and both endure it. In order to thrive, we have to understand prolonged enduring. We must be able to articulate it. Only then can anxiety and negativity be managed. Until we can talk about this, we can't position ourselves to get past it. In our talking, we have to build a bigger door together so that the elephant in the room, our history of slavery, can find a place to move about more freely.

Self-giving also promotes a sense of accomplishment that results in an even greater willingness to give. When we think about that, we realize that the sense of accomplishment that results from self-giving comes from what we must endure when we are on this imaginary boat that we call life.

Every day presents us with situations where we can choose to be givers or takers. For example, there is nothing wrong with honestly taking what is yours when you are at work. In that situation, you have a sense of a place and time being yours, and you take your stand with a sense of responsibility. There are some folks on the boat of life who are not self-giving. As a matter of fact, some want to take what is yours. I think this is something that many people miss most about themselves. The result of this selfishness is what causes much of the volatility and chaos that we see so much today. People want to be recognized for what they do give, what they contribute, too. A lack of proper thanks for those who give is also something we as a society are beginning to see. If there is nothing else I learned in almost thirty-four years of pastoring, I learned how sensitive people are about being properly recognized for what they do give.

No matter how we define satisfaction - I will refer to it as joy - we find that some folks want to take our joy, another person's joy, and even the joy of people down the street. They want it all for themselves, whether they want recognition, money, or their own way. Part of that is because self-giving has not turned into an understanding of what it means to properly receive. I say this as a warning for us all. Until we learn how to receive, we really can't give.

During my time as a pastoral supervisor, I told more than one pastor that until we learn how to receive, we never truly learn how to give. This is an important aspect of relating to one another. Until we learn how to give to our communities, we won't know how to receive. Until we learn how to give in our community organizations, our colleges, or any other setting, we won't know how to receive. It becomes a circular process in that we are free to receive as we've become freed to give, and that freedom of giving results in the ability to receive yet again.

When you are really free to look in that mirror and ask yourself who you are, you have the ability to come away in a very positive state of mind. When you understand prolonged enduring, you can fully embrace the positivity that comes from that enduring as found in verses 4 and 5 of Psalms 30, from the English Standard Version that reads, *"Sing praises to the Lord all ye saints and give thanks to His holy name for His anger is but for a moment and His favor is for a lifetime. Weeping may tarry for the night but joy comes with the morning."*

I have always used scripture to explain the joy that comes after the prolonged enduring. I often think about a pastor who helped me with this concept. He related it in a way that I understood as living in the land of opposition. He also found that it had a great deal to do with his own self-understanding. He explained that many of us are weeping and may tarry for a night that becomes many, many more.

We have to be very careful in our ability to remain steady because prolonged enduring is not always just for a night. It could be for many, many more. Realizing this enables us to stay on the boat and understand ourselves even as we know that while some may weep for one night, others may weep much longer.

There is also the need to understand that prolonged enduring is a voyage with an ending that is not easily predicted. With a sense of selflessness and self-giving however, comes the knowledge that each effort we make to give freely to others will contribute to a more enjoyable trip, or a bon voyage, for us all.

## CHAPTER 5 – FINDING HOPE IN BEING
## All Hands on Deck

Chapter Five is about finding hope in being, with the underscore of the nautical vernacular of "General quarters, general quarters! All hands on deck!" I was not blessed to serve in the United States Navy but had help with the language from my friend, Master Chief Ivria Johnson, Jr., who shared some appropriate phrasing. Others also helped with this along the way.

"All hands on deck" means that we all report, and quickly, when that particular call comes. The phrase is called when a lot of work is to be done in a short amount of time, when a situation demands that everyone report. Also, we find hope in that call. It means we have work to do to make sure we stay together because remember, we are all on the same boat. We could also liken this to the literary world and William Shakespeare's quote, "To be or not to be, that is the question." What we will be, and what that means, is the concept that drove my desire to write this book.

Quite simply, everyone needs to do something, to try to encourage others to do something, and to create a sense of urgency that results in action. Finding hope in being called to action is relevant because it means it is time for us to come together to accomplish something. This hope falls across all circles of life. A school child can comprehend it and should be fully able to implement it by grade twelve, if not earlier. This concept is for that supervisor who for so many days, months and years has just been going to work and letting things happen as they do without ever sounding the alarm to take action. This also applies to the religious world. Some are us are doing a really bad job of spreading a really good message of hope. We can go to philosophy for that hope, or Christianity, which I believe has much to offer to us all. Regardless of the approach, I think we are doing a bad job of getting that message of hope to people, that being or not being, that call for action.

The current call of hope is that it is time for us "to be." I will relate to this in terms of office, place or position. When I was a district superintendent, I sent letters to all lay persons and asked that they remember to respect the office of the pastor. I explained that while we may not care for the individual, it is important to respect the office, the position. When I think about the concept of being called to action, I think of it in the same way, in certain times, places and phases of life.

For example, it is important to respect the time of being a child, which on its face may be hard to comprehend. There are certain ways of behaving as a child that shaped my being. Children didn't normally speak until adults told them to or otherwise engaged them. I had to understand that to be a child. If I moved from this tenet of being a child, it was assumed that I moved to a place where I did not know what to do or how to perform. I could not be a teenager or young adult and participate in the conversations of those we referred to as "grown folks." This may run counter to what some do in their home, and I understand that. In our home, we tried to raise our children to understand their position. They were not to speak when adults were speaking. It is not that the children were not to say anything. They were to wait for the appropriate time, to be children. Shakespeare's quote is clear in this regard.

As children grow older, they continue on their quest of being. I will use playing on a baseball team as an example because I played baseball. Sports, like other organized activities, have definite roles and responsibilities for everyone involved. To be the pitcher in a game means we couldn't be the catcher or the first baseman. To try to play multiple positions is problematic, something we have likely seen in many young children, quite possibly our own. There will always be at least one child on the baseball field who will try to catch the ball and run over to tag the runner, who wants to play all the positions. When others will not let us play our role or be in our position, we often want to jump off the boat.

As we grow older, we become teenagers. Later, we attend high school. Many of us continue to learn a trade or attend college, also things connected to the idea of being. There was something particular about my college education that I still remember. At Philander Smith College, I learned that I was a citizen of the world. It's not that I never felt or failed to recognize the discrepancies at that time between colleges. What I knew then and know to this day is that Philander Smith College is fully accredited and recognized as an institutional member of the North Central Association of Colleges and Schools. I felt that the college education I received was equivalent to that offered at any college in the United States. We were encouraged to be world citizens, to be able to relate to others anywhere in this country or overseas.

To be able to relate to others, it is important to know your position, and to know where you are. When you know that, you are able to articulate who you are and what you are meant to be in such a way that makes it easier to stay on boat. It also makes it easier for others to stay on with you. When I was blessed to go to seminary in 1982, one of the faculty at the Saint Paul School of Theology in Kansas City, Missouri, said something I will never forget. He pounded into me the idea of being a world citizen and what that meant. I had written a paper that was somewhat colloquial, or narrow in scope. It may have been too regional. Even though I was going to school in the middle west, I likely wrote it from a southern perspective, and from that of an African American as well. I'm not sure of all the details, but I remember what my professor told me about it. "Whatever you write at the Saint Paul School of Theology may be read by anyone around the world," he said.

When I think about the internet phenomenon and social media today, it occurs to me that people get on the internet and perhaps don't realize that what they write goes around the world. We should be able to write so that regardless of our location, people can relate to what is written. I learned that during my undergraduate and graduate school years as well as my time in seminary. I understood that I was a world citizen, and that what I wrote could be critiqued wherever there was access to what I had written. That was very empowering to me and also caused me to think of myself as a fence builder, which involves a state of being. To be a fence builder and citizen of the world gives us a sense of being that defines us from the theological perspective that we learn in the Bible and sing in the hymn, "I Shall Not Be Moved."

I have been blessed in all the different jobs I have held. I worked in a manufacturing plant once where my job was to buff portable aluminum kitchens. They were similar in finish to that of barbeque grills. To be a good buffer, I had to buff each portable kitchen after it came out of the mold, to make it smooth. I took great pride in buffing those portable kitchens until they were fully smooth, too. When I was a letter carrier, I tried to be a good letter carrier, to make sure folks got their mail. That sense of being we achieve when we are absorbed in the work we do happens when we have a good understanding of what it means to be - and not to be - in a particular role with certain responsibilities. As I look at how we determine who we will be to get our task done, we must first know our role, whether we are co-workers, employees, or supervisors.

Supervisors have to understand why and how they make the adjustments they do to get work done. My son was a manager for a retail store at one time. The store generated two or three-million dollars a year, and was generating a good profit. I understood what this meant when I related it to my work as a letter carrier at the post office. A supervisor indicated how many hours would have to be worked that week to get the mail carried. In that retail store, my son knew how many hours had to be worked at what labor cost to generate an expected profit margin. Good managers make sure they schedule work within a specified time frame, at a certain cost, to get the work done.

I remember a day at the post office that was providential. Surely the Lord was involved! The postmaster came over and was talking to my immediate supervisor. My supervisor was talking about the volume of mail to be delivered and his concern about getting it done within the week with the labor available, when the postmaster said, "Well, if you can't get the mail carried, then you've got to carry it yourself." Whenever there is a job to be done, I think supervisors must make decisions to make work happen. One way to do that is to make adjustments to ensure the work is done well, and on schedule. Supervisors can also do some of the work themselves when necessary. They must take on that extra load. This is one way to empower workers. Employees will have more confidence in how supervisors make decisions, and supervisor will get much better results, if they can be in their position and work side-by-side with those they supervise. The adjustment-making process that supervisors go through often leads to comradery, a bonding with others in the workplace that brings everyone closer.

Experience as a supervisor helps us lead in a way that makes everyone feel connected, no matter what the position. This connection puts an equal value on the role of both the supervisor and the co-worker. We affirm co-workers when we show by our actions that there is no small job. In truth, all work is important and necessary to achieve the goal. This affirms everyone. Supervisors make the adjustments, bond with their employees, and then affirm them so they feel that they must be in their role to make work happen. Whether I was a letter carrier, a city employee, a pastor, or a paint mixer at a Sherwin Williams Paint Store, I was part of the whole, and I took action.

Everything I said about the role of supervisor can be incorporated into any enterprise. We know we are all there to take action when at the end of an eight-hour day, someone says, "I didn't even realize the day had flown by like that, and that we had accomplished what we set out to do." At the end of the work or school day, the end of the worship service meeting, this feeling makes a big difference. So, Shakespeare's "to be or not to be" is always the question, and the call of "all hands on deck" creates the sense of urgency in those who have the skill and sense of empowerment to complete the work, from top to bottom.

"All hands on deck" means that we are all in this together, and that we are ready "to be."

## CHAPTER 6 – THE REALITY OF MINORITY
**Single Up**

This is a transitional chapter. It falls in the middle of the eleven chapters of this book, and it moves us in a different direction. We are now talking about what I will refer to as the ocean of life. We are floating on this very massive body of water that we can't control, even as we have often managed to isolate ourselves to the point that we sometimes think we have more impact than we do. In nautical terms, it is time to "single up," or to prepare to get underway with mooring lines that serve to double our safety against breaking free from a single line.

We don't know what will happen on the ocean of life, not even for a moment. During the time today that I am working on this book, there have been tragic accidents and significant events. Just three years ago, the world was introduced Pope Francis of the Roman Catholic Church, on March 13, 2013. He is a significant world leader, and I hope that the totality of his ministry and his work for this world is successful.

The title of this chapter is "The Reality of Minority." However, I don't want to personalize this chapter by restricting it to being relatable to African Americans alone. Whether we like it or not, when we think only of our individual reality, we become so involved in what we are communicating that people can miss our point. I want to broaden the context of what minority means.

Being a minority is a reality, and there is nothing wrong with that. There are positives that come from being a minority. Minorities can bring the voice and perspective of their existence and that of others in their group to those different from themselves. Minorities have their own destiny, one that often finds them sailing far beyond where others might place them. You remember I talked earlier about the isms out there. We could be affected by any one of them including classism, racism, ageism or sexism. Discrimination also affects those with disabilities or those who are part of the LGBT&Q community. All of us, regardless of gender, color, race, politics, religion or sexual identity can find ourselves in places where we are the minority.

I think I can personalize my next point because I am an African American who thinks that in certain settings. some African Americans try not to be identified as such. I think they do this through choices about where they live, worship, or spend their social time. The reality is that if you are an African American, you will always be so. There was a time in this country when some African Americans who, due to the light color of their skin, would be able to do what many of us call "cross." Rather than be identified as African American, these people passed themselves off as white. They crossed over and lived the white life. They did not face the reality of being African American in very difficult times, and they denied themselves and others within their race in doing so.

There is no way I would pass for white. I wouldn't pass for Asian, and I wouldn't pass for any of the brown races, either. I am a very dark African American, and I have to deal with issues even within my own race because of that darkness. If we use the boat scenario and think of the animals, we know that only two of each species, one female and one male, were brought aboard. Each pair was a majority within themselves, but they were a minority of the whole. In that sense, we are all minorities at some point.

Well-known American writer Mark Twain said, "Whenever you find yourself on the side of the minority, it is time to pause and reflect." These are very profound words. When we find ourselves in the minority, taking the time to pause and reflect is part of how we stay on the boat. I would ask those who are reading this to pause when you are the minority, because pausing is a good thing. As a matter of fact, pausing may be preferable to stopping; when we stop, there is an end. When we pause, we continue and are still on the journey. Remember, we must have a journey mentality. I think that many times when we find ourselves on the side of minority and feel the reality of that, we fail to pause and may regret missing that opportunity. My sons, my daughter, and my daughters-in-law have all tried to help me with this. They are very good at taking time to pause and reflect before they react.

My son once talked to me about his approach. He found that when in the minority, we must define that and use it in a sentence we speak to ourselves, so that we have an example that can help us to articulate it. Many times I have come through that pause to find I must also identify the setting and its impact. I have to explain that to myself, that it makes sense for me to stay where I am because I belong. I have to look myself in the mirror and reflect on who I am, and talk about it with my partner or someone I can trust as I process what has occurred. To do this allows us to remain confident in ourselves as we stay on the boat, and it works no matter where we are. We need to pause after we find ourselves in that minority setting. We have to talk about it, too. Then, we can deal with the reality of it and can often come to very positive feelings about ourselves and our journey. I'm going to push Mark Twain's quote a little further, and suggest that we pause, reflect, and then ask questions.

If there is nothing else in my life that has been good for me, I can say that the training that the church gave me inspired me to ask questions. My father, Thelma McAdoo, said time and again, "There's no such thing as a dumb question," something I've repeated to my kids. When dealing with the reality of being a minority we need to pause, reflect, talk about the situation, and ask questions. In her book *Extraordinary Ordinary People. A Memoir of Family*," former United States Secretary of State, Dr. Condoleezza Rice, said, "It's good to have female minority role models, but the important thing is to have mentors who care about you, and they come in all colors." I think what Dr. Rice said is important. We need role models and mentors, regardless of their race or gender, to help us realize that the person who brings us relief may not be a mirror reflection of ourselves.

I am sure that during the forty days on Noah's Ark, those aboard found mentors different from themselves. I really think that it is a true blessing to find a mentor, whether that individual is similar to you or not. We must truly understand how important it is to be around someone who can enrich us in those settings when we know we are the minority. There is no way we can get around it. What we can do instead of wallowing in the negative aspects of that reality is to be thankful for the positive aspects of being there. And when we are in the minority, we must be aware of the level of that.

Sometimes those in the minority are plainly evident through their gender. As women move into board rooms and other places they have not been before, they face both a male-dominated way of conducting business and the feelings that come from being different. As diversity in race and gender increases, those with feelings of difference will find themselves becoming more comfortable.

I will close this chapter with a quote from one of my favorite theologians, Soren Kierkegaard, who said, "Truth always rests with the minority, and the minority is always stronger than the majority, because the majority is generally formed by those who really have an opinion, while the strength of a minority is illusory, formed by the gangs who have no opinion--and who, therefore, in the next instant (when it is evident that the minority is the stronger) assumes its opinion…while Truth again reverts to a new minority."

What Kierkegaard is saying to me is that the state of minority is a sociological, psychological process. It is also something we can see throughout our history. The illusion he mentions is maintained by the majority to force compliance. It consists of beliefs, spoken words and behavior by those in authority, as was the case of those who said that slaves, the minority, preferred being enslaved. It took abolitionists who were in the minority- and a Civil War - to begin the long road to African American freedom.

The women's suffrage movement was similar in that women, while a sizable minority, were held firmly in place as secondary to men, and were denied the right to vote and other civil liberties. Every civil rights movement begins with an enforced compliance that is changed by those who work to change the majority. As women and other minorities single up, they double their strength and impact, and can move forward to create the next new Truth.

# CHAPTER 7 – STEPS  /ARD  BOAT-STAYING TRANSITION

## Land Ho!

I began preaching in 1980, and I left for seminary in 1982. My Christian history professor, Dr. Carl Bangs, said that change was the hardest thing to deal with in the churches we would pastor. That didn't register much with me then. I was naïve like a lot of folks who thought that because the Lord had called us to preach the gospel, we were theological geniuses. We soon found out that was not the case.

Another professor, Dr. Lindsey Pheigo, told me early in my seminary days that my theology was encased in concrete. He also said it was going to be the job of the seminary faculty to jackhammer away at that concrete so that my theology would not remain as hardened as it was when I arrived. I say this to remind everyone that land will be sighted at the time of boat-staying transition, but my arrival at seminary did not mean anyone was ready to shout "land ho," a phrase that means that land is in sight. We should look at our boat-staying transition that way. We have not arrived. We are only preparing to land at this stage, and there is still work to be done to get there.

We may not have been aware of it at the time, but we started taking steps to land the minute we arrived at seminary, just as we all do in any organized endeavor. I have focused so far on what is required to stay on the boat together, but remember that there will be a place to depart, so we've got to prepare. You knew we had to get off that boat at some point!

Dr. Bangs was also trying to tell us that some people don't want to get off the boat. This brings me back to Einstein's Theory of Relativity. Nothing stays the same. Life is not stagnant. To prepare to get off the boat, we experience transition. Transition will happen whether we prepare for it or not.

Change happens in every age group, in all facets of our lives. We work, go to school, and worship with others in churches, synagogues, mosques, or temples. Change occurs no matter where we find ourselves. Everyone and everything around us impacts how we change.

As a child of the sixties, I remember Sam Cooke's song, "A Change Is Gonna Come." This chapter is going to deal with that change, and how those of us on the boat have to realize that we are going to have to get off the boat one day. This is not always easy for us to understand. It is easy to become comfortable, even sedentary, not only in our bodies, but in our minds. I learned early on that the easy way to be a pastoral supervisor would be to tell some church congregations to keep doing what they had been doing the last forty years. Those churches would be as happy as they could be. If I went to these congregations and talked about change, the reaction would be quite different.

Change is easier for those who understand that once again, we are all in this together. Transitional changes impact our lives and the lives of those around us. The question is what we make of these changes, and how we transition. We are going to have to respond at any rate. To remain stagnant is no way to prepare.

Let's talk about change from an academic prospective. I believe that every day is a day to learn something. Learning means to change, to add new skills and increase understanding. Appreciation for that change should be instilled in us from preschool through high school, and beyond. There should be an appreciation for learning throughout our lives. I want to continue to change, to learn more about English, math, and science, every day. I have changed through thirty-four years in ministry, fifteen years of work in government agencies that included two years in the military, and ownership of a business. If we realize that change is a reality and apply that knowledge to our lives, we can prepare for our feelings about it. Even so, change is not always easy. I struggle with it myself.

Focusing on change and preparing for it makes it easier for me to move forward.

I mentioned commas in an earlier chapter and said that we should look at them as pauses, places to slow down and reflect. I discussed periods as places to end sentences, or to end our journey. Commas occur throughout our lives, and we need to recognize them as points where change occurs. When they come, we must shift in order to make the transition to the next point.

When I was a letter carrier with the United States Postal Service, changes in population could result in changes in route assignments. Politics could be behind those changes and how they were implemented, but that is true in any work setting. What is important to note is that if you are still doing the same thing at work that you were doing twenty years ago and there has been no significant change in the work, you are in trouble. A church that hasn't seen any change in the last fifteen or twenty years is in jeopardy, too. If you are in academia and still teaching the same information and providing the same ways for students to learn, you are also in trouble. Your students are poorly served, too.

I wrote earlier about ways to handle anxiety or panic. Teachers along the way gave me other techniques that I have tried throughout the years. One is to remain aware that we are all in this together, and that nobody jumped off the boat. We picked up relational skills along the way, during our time on the boat. We learned to interact with others and to learn from them, and we learned how to remain steady when both people and situations around us seemed unsteady. We continue to learn in the middle of the ocean of life.

When preparing to get off the boat and transition to a new direction, we should also note that we picked up some communication skills along the way. We are constantly learning how to communicate with others. We discover through each communication what works in that situation, and what does not. Teachers must be able to communicate with students, and students learn to communicate through interaction with their teachers. Early on in this book, I talked about my home life as a child, the way I grew up. I hope I have expressed the importance of learning and of staying in school, something that I believe good parents instill in their children early in life. Mine did that for me, and I am grateful.

Asking questions is vital to effective communication. If I am able to speak on my death bed, I will probably ask the doctor a question about my situation, which harkens back to my father's teaching. He told me early on that there is no such thing as a stupid question. If you have a question at work, school or church, ask it! I have asked questions throughout my career, at every job or point of service. If I did not know something or did not understand, I asked a question. As a teacher, a member of the work force, and particularly through my years of pastoring, I have determined that the biggest problem today is that people don't ask enough questions.

If we ask the questions, the answers are there. Did you hear what I said? The answers are there. They may not be the answers that we want to hear, but the answers are there. They may not be absolute or perfect, but they are available. Information gives us an opportunity to impact decision-making, or to at least know more about how decisions that impact us are made. When getting off the boat, we've got to make sure that we continue to ask the right questions. We practiced communication on the boat, and will continue to develop this skill as long as we live.

My work has taken me to a variety of settings, and I had to deal with neighbors in each one. Neighbors are important people to understand. I've been blessed to have good neighbors everywhere I lived, but I also found that conflict is a part of any relationship, as is the need to have the skills to resolve it. Some of my neighbors and I had conflicts about my dog. I will never forget one neighbor who said, "I am getting tired of walking across my yard and stepping in this dog stuff. Neighbor, something's got to give." And something did give. We got rid of the dog. That may be difficult for some people to understand, but I wasn't going to let the dog come between my neighbor and me. Good communication also promotes understanding. We develop empathy as we consider the concerns of others.

Communication is a two-way street that can be very crooked and curved, with slopes and hills, or smooth and straight, with few obstacles. I would imagine that the people on Noah's Ark found themselves on both sides of that. Throughout this book, I have presented communication as a way to get things done. Communication is important when dealing with differences between men and women, something that I am sure people on the boat also knew.

I have been married forty-six years to my dear wife, Gloria, but it took me about twenty years before I had enough sense to say, "I didn't hear you. What did you say?" when I was leaving the house. I guess it dawned on me that I should do that after I came back from the store so many times to hear, "I told you to get (whatever the item I didn't return with was) as you were walking out the door." The truth is, my wife most likely did tell me everything that she wanted, but I didn't always hear her. Then, there might have been an argument over it. Now, as I am leaving the house and think I hear everything, I stop and say, "I didn't hear you. What did you say?" While we are on the boat and in this together, we've got to listen to one another. Gloria and I are on this boat forever, and I am blessed in that.

One way to approach effective listening is to realize that you can't talk and listen at the same time. I am an extrovert and a talker, something everyone who knows me can confirm. This can be a problem, too, because people like me are often thinking about what they are going to say next instead of listening to the other person talking. I am trying to improve my listening skills by deliberately listening instead of anticipating my turn to talk. I need to focus on the speaker instead of preparing my next comment. I also recommend asking questions as part of effective listening, to make sure you understand what has been said.

In academia, we learn through communication between teacher and student. Teachers also teach us how to communicate with others. There are protocols of communication in school. In elementary school, we learn that teachers set the rules and standards that we will go by. As we move through elementary school, there is more dialogue between teachers and students, but the dialogue is conducted in a prescribed fashion. We learn how to be called on for answers, and how to answer correctly. In both middle school and high school, communication begins to become a dialogue that operates on an understood contract of expectations that shouldn't require as much from either side.

Many standards that we learn in school are implied. By middle school, students adhere to a type of contract. They should arrive on time and be ready to sit down and learn. Teachers start class on time and communicate what is to be covered that day. These implied contracts continue as we work our way through school. For those who continue to vocational training or college, it is expected that instructors and professors communicate what is to be done, and students participate through dialogue, assignments, and reading. Learning is an active process.

We must ask questions about faith and spirituality, too. I think it is a sin to be too quiet in church. Asking questions is vital to effective communication from both sides of the pulpit. One of the things my son, Charlie McAdoo II, always says to me is that quiet mouths don't get fed. In some religious circles, people who say they aren't being fed at their church are referring to their spiritual fulfillment. I hear this frequently. People say they aren't being fed, fulfilled, or uplifted by their church experience. We should ask these folks if they have defined the specific problem. If not, they could go to another church and discover that they are unfulfilled there as well. It is important to ask ourselves what is happening in this instance, where is the gap they are experiencing.

Perhaps the feeling is that the preacher can't preach well, or he or she doesn't pray well with the congregation. Others may think that the pastor isn't as effective in day-to-day pastoring as they would like. It is important to remember that no pastor is perfect. None of us is equally strong in all aspects of our work, so it should not be a surprise when a pastor may be weaker in some pastoral skills. Frankly, there are great pastors who can't preach a lick, not a lick, but they are doing their very best.

My dear friend, Mr. Ivria Johnson, Jr., told me a story once that reminds me of the work of a pastor and how it is often judged. Ivria's condition had slowed him down a bit, something he was talking about one day as I drove him to a doctor's appointment. He asked me if I had ever been out in the fields and been the one driving the tractor that takes folks home in the evening. I told him I had never done that. "Well," he said, "This is how it works. We have worked all day, and I'm the person who is driving the tractor when everybody is trying to get home to do something that evening. They all want me to go faster, but I've got the tractor wide open. I've got my foot as far down as the pedal will go. I am doing the very best that I can." So when I go to get Ivria and he's not ready and says, "I've got the pedal down to the floor. I'm doing the very best I can," I understand him. As is the case with many pastors, Ivria is doing all that he can to get us there.

Pastors often stay in the same pastorate for twenty-five or thirty years because the people in their church see they are doing the very best they can to build God's kingdom. God has called all of us, the congregation included, to be part of the ministry of the church. God did so knowing that He gave different attributes to pastors and congregants, all to make the congregation whole.

In the religious world, if we don't ask ourselves why we feel as if we aren't being fed, we are probably not looking for the cafeteria line and the choices it offers. By this I mean that even if that pastor can't do everything as well as we would like, people still find their way to that church, and to that pastor. They choose what they prefer from what is offered, and they are often more satisfied.

In the world of business and organizational management, effective communication is a basic expectation. When I worked at the paint factory, our daily objective was to produce a certain kind and quantity of paint. My bosses didn't often talk to us in such a way that instilled pride and affirmation of doing a good job of producing paint. When I worked in the factory making portable kitchens, my boss rarely came by to talk about the work I was doing, or to affirm that the portable kitchens had smooth surfaces after production. Affirmation and pride in doing a good job was something that had to come from within.

Because this particular chapter is about getting off the boat and effectively communicating with one another, I want to talk about the importance of affirming others, and the sense of pride that comes from that affirmation. Industry has come to understand this. I believe the business world is doing more and more to affirm both their employees and their importance in meeting the goal. Supervisors and staff are being trained to be more open, to engage in conversation, and to talk about topics that bring value to the work environment. If everyone in the company at every level, from the employees to the executive level, is communicating about the way to provide the best product possible, change for the better will result. While we are still working for ourselves to some extent, there is a pyramid of positive mentality that comes from working toward the goal and appreciating everyone. This positivity is better for all involved. Remember, we are all in this together. Even as we work for ourselves, we should represent the area in which we work as best we can to meet our goals.

The military has a form of communication, a specific chain of command. Information flows both up and down the chain, but authority runs from top to bottom. The hierarchy in the military is very clear. If you relate this chain of command to Noah's Ark, however, you could stipulate that everyone had equal authority. No decision could be made on the boat that could overrule others. God was in control of the boat and everyone on it, and there was no power higher. His was the ultimate authority.

The best communication occurs when everyone at every level of an organization has the ability to communicate with others, regardless of position. As a matter of fact, hierarchical lines in some places have become so confused that many of us have trouble communicating. Remember that this is a journey book. No one can explain everything that might occur when we get off the boat.

I want to quote something one of my sons, Leron Charles McAdoo, said about attaining knowledge. We were discussing how knowledge can make a difference. According to Leron, "Knowledge is a tool that can be used for good or for evil." Again, according to Leron, "Knowledge is a tool that can be used for good or evil." Let's consider an example. We agree that a hammer is a tool that can be used to build something. That same hammer can also be used to hurt someone. It can be used for good or for evil. The hammer can be used to build or to destroy.

Education is also a tool. It's not an end or a guarantee of what is to come. It is a tool that can be used for good or bad. There are people with a great deal of knowledge that know more about their particular field of interest than others will ever know. But if that knowledge isn't transferable, is there life in it? If it can't be used by someone else or applied for someone else's benefit, is it alive? Knowledge, without the ability to transfer or use it to help others, is a dead entity. Knowledge is a tool that I think is sometimes gained by people who fail to apply it productively. We hear much about how smart some people are, particularly in the areas of math and science. Both areas provide career possibilities that are very sought after these days.

The Lord has blessed me with grandchildren, one of whom is in the teen years. We have another rapidly approaching that point. Knowledge alone will not help adolescents with the problems of growing up that occur outside the classroom. Knowledge alone will not help teenagers weaving through physical and emotional changes and life lessons to find their way to adulthood. Knowledge of any kind is a tool that can be applied as we grow, but it is not the only one. None of us moves though this world on knowledge alone.

I think this is where we have been failing our children. We have stressed so much the importance of obtaining the knowledge to conjugate verbs, to solve science problems in the lab, or to achieve A's, that we are doing them an injustice. My children would come home from school and expound on algebra, geometry or the like, the higher mathematics. "I may not know mathematics, but I know arithmetic," is often my response. The knowledge of a faster way to do complicated problems is fine, but we still need to confidently add, subtract, multiply and divide, and to know what the results mean. At the end of the day, I'm still going to be able to get to the same answer they do, although it may take me a bit longer.

In my opinion, mathematics is now approached as something that focuses on computer technology, the quickest way to an answer. Understanding the steps involved in mathematics is equally as important as what each number means. Otherwise, we are in a hurry going nowhere. I repeat. We are in a hurry going nowhere when we rush along just to rush along to get done, or in this case, get the answer. When we depart from the boat and get out in the world, we should not rush. We should take time to determine what is going on around us. Knowledge alone won't give us that. Often, knowledge prepares us to think before we accept the first answer that comes along.

In both the religious and secular world, we have placed such a high value on knowledge for its own sake that some tend to be better at quoting scripture than understanding it. Although it was twenty years ago, I will never forget something that was said to me in a Sunday school class shortly after I returned from seminary. There was a discussion about a theological point and when I didn't respond with an immediate answer, someone said, "You didn't learn that in seminary?" We covered about two thousand years of theological understanding during seminary, and it would be difficult to recall everything covered.

Frankly, I am less interested in how many verses of the Bible people can quote than I am in how they treat their brothers and sisters. How are you treating your family? How are you treating the people in the church? How are you treating your co-workers, your community members, or your neighbors? Do you serve those in need? While it is good to have that knowledge base of biblical quotes to drawn upon, it is more valuable if that knowledge has a positive impact on what you do.

To quote the Bible extensively, to know the location and context of those verses, the secondary languages of Greek, Hebrew and Arabic is all wonderful, but are we living them? Are there hungry people in the world to be fed, or prisoners to be visited? Are we doing what it takes to move our knowledge of Christ to the next level? I believe that Biblical knowledge, like any other, is a tool for good or for evil. The fact that some folks use it just to hit other folks over the head with it proves my point.

In the work world, knowledge is of value and can provide a point from which to negotiate our importance, authority and salary. Many hoard their work knowledge for that very reason. They feel more secure in their positions if they keep what they know to themselves. Knowledge, even in the industrial or technological setting, is best used in ways that give the people who apply that knowledge a real sense of meaning and contribution. I was just home in Tennessee recently with Jerry Oldham, a cousin of mine who had worked in industry, in manufacturing. He had recently retired because of health issues, and was at home when a former company colleague called him from a candy factory. He told me about it, and said he loved getting that call, too. The company representative said, "The candy we are running ain't doing right." My cousin told him that they needed to increase the temperature five degrees and cool the candy twenty seconds less than they were actually cooling it. He also told him to call back if that didn't work. While the machine itself was doing what it was supposed to do, my cousin knew and loved the candy industry. His experience had taught him that even if the machine was working properly, a couple of slight adjustments would make the candy better. His knowledge of how the technology actually worked proved more important than the technology itself.

So, I have gone from communication to candy. Why would anyone want to read this book? Why would a supervisor want to read this book? Well, we all want to make a better batch of candy, a better computer or chair, or a service that provides a better way of life. We do things better when we understand that while the knowledge we have is good, we have to understand how to apply it to make a real difference.

As I stated earlier, knowledge of the subject to be taught is important for teachers. It is equally important that they know their students. Good teachers need to know a little bit about the interests of each generation of students they are teaching. Each brings different expectations and experiences. This information helps everyone who is preparing those students to get off the boat, by the way.

But I have another comment to make, to my cousin, Mitchell Moore. The Bible doesn't say anything about it in the Noah story, but there had to be some people coming off the boat who were peace breakers. No matter what we are doing, there will always be peace breakers. They are the people that my cousin, Michael, was talking about with me. Peace breakers just are not happy when things are going smoothly. Many of the peace breakers know they can get under someone's skin by breaking the peace, causing some sort of disruption with a comment or a glance. Peace breakers know who they can irritate. Teachers have certain students that get under their skin, too. You teachers will be doing fine until you walk into the classroom and see a peace breaker. Suddenly, you find yourself wondering if you can leave for the day.

I pastored for thirty-four years and I had some church members that I wished would not show up to meetings because they were just peace breakers. This is a reality. Getting off the boat doesn't mean that everything will be easy. I have supervised over two-hundred churches and worked with both preachers and laity. As a parent, I often found myself in the role of peace keeper. I hope that I also served my children more often as a peace maker than a peace keeper. I see the role of peace keeper as one who does the minimum to keep order, which is a temporary step designed to stop disorder without building  harmony and understanding. I hope I taught my children, by example, the importance of being a peace maker. Those who make peace can help others understand the importance of granting peace to others, another way to realize that we are all in this together.

Our successful transition to land is dependent on leaving the boat and dealing with those who break our peace. Preparing to transition means to become a peace maker, one who deals with others in ways that benefit all involved. Thus ends Chapter Seven. Land Ho!

## CHAPTER 8 – 21ST CEN      Y INCLUSIVENESS WE ARE ALL SHIPMA

I offer this chapter as a way to cool down, much like a transition that comes after significant effort or exercise. It is offered to enable us to have a different view of others from what we may have at present. This will help us transition to our future together.

According to United States Census data, the white majority in the United States will become a minority by 2043. The eventual deaths of the baby boomer generation, combined with the growing rates of the Hispanic population, will find that African Americans, Hispanics and other people of color will become the majority before the twenty-second century. Those who are in the minority now, myself included, should be aware of that and steadfast in our Christian perspective through this transition of minority to majority. We are all God's children, and I believe that God is going to be with us regardless of the demographics of our country. It will be critical that we think of others through a mindset of positivity.

Remember that the essence of being on the boat for forty days was that those on the boat had to deal with what I referred to earlier as opposites, those different from themselves. When we understand that, we can look at

66

people in another light, one in which we think of them as similar to us. If we look at it from that perspective and not one of opposition, people different from ourselves can be thought of as others, rather than as opposites. In fact, others are just that. Others are human beings who also have to live in this world. We all deserve the right to pursue education to work to support our families.  Like us, others also deserve the opportunity to develop their understanding of God, or the spiritual base or force that moves their lives forward. In that regard, we are shipmates.

This chapter focuses on examining how we look at those different from ourselves.  After all, each of us is unique. I will start with the concept of positive difference. It is often the case that when we look at anything different from what we have previously experienced, we tend to see it in a negative light and even with suspicion. Wouldn't it be wonderful if instead we could look at people different from ourselves as those who bring a positive difference?

I will begin by discussing inanimate objects, say cars or trucks.  While some people prefer a Ford, others prefer a Chevrolet or another brand until someone drives up in a different vehicle. Imagine that you are the one driving the Ford, and another person drives up in a Chevrolet. You are firm in your opinion that your Ford is a superior product but you are open to what you might learn about the Chevrolet. As you talk with the Chevrolet owner, you learn more about the car.  You discover that with new technology, the Chevrolet is a very nice vehicle that you would consider as a future purchase. Through interaction, you gained perspective about the other person's vehicle. This is similar to what can occur when we meet people for the first time.  If we look at them with an appreciation for difference rather than through feelings of suspicion or negativity, we are much more likely to see them in positive light.

I have tried to impress upon my children that they should think less about what some refer to as life style. I think life style is really a misnomer. Life style is evident by appearance and defined by others, often those in advertising, by what we drive or where we live. Instead, I tried to teach my children to think about a life way, something that is not defined by external influences. A life way is self-directed and has little to do with such things as cars and homes. A life way is about our values, and how we live our lives through them.

A life way is about how we approach others. What are our values as related to the way we should treat other human beings? Should those values be based on skin color or suspicion? As I discussed in previous chapters, we are all in the minority at some point. If we look at this question from the perspective of positive difference, we can begin to broaden our scope. Difference simply means not the same in some aspect. The negativity we sometimes attach to that difference narrows our perspective. Negativity impacts our ability to relate to one another, and it also allows us to forget that we are all in this together.

There are so many positives in the difference that others bring to our lives! When met with an open mind, differences in culture often result in sincere appreciation. I'm reminded of some of my friends from England who always observe their daily tea time. What a lovely idea! Friends of mine from Mexico have siesta time, something that was different from my experience but has been found to have merit. Doctors and scientists find validity in the idea that a short rest period during the day promotes better health and increases alertness.

One of the things I regret not having offered in my ministry was a vesper time. Maybe because I could relate to the concept to tea time in London and siesta time in Mexico, I wanted to offer my congregation fifteen or twenty minutes to transition from late afternoon to early evening. I wanted parishioners leaving work a chance to stop in at church to relax before they rushed home. I wanted to provide them time to acknowledge life beyond school, work, evening chores, television or even Sunday services. People are busy, especially those with children. It appeared that there was no way to squeeze in what I think would have been be a very beneficial time for them. This time of deliberate transition hasn't been a part of America's Christian church culture, but wouldn't it be wonderful if it could be?

To appreciate others means to expand our own church memberships. If we aren't bringing new people in, we are going to decrease in number until no one is there. The thing to remember is that we have all this, and heaven, too. We have our lives on earth and the opportunity to experience others, and that should be considered a plus. When we see interacting with others as a negative experience, our faces and bodies change to a closed stance.

Our personal well-being depends on interaction with others. When we interact with open minds and hearts, our faces and bodies change to reflect positivity and peace. Just think of what that does for the way each of us interacts on earth! Remember those who were on Noah's Ark? They were with people they didn't know. We have to determine to make the transition of seeing others as positive rather than seeing others as opposite from ourselves. This is our responsibility. Those who value others and go into situations with an eye toward difference as a positive know that we are all in this together. When we determine that we will see others in this way, we open channels of communication wherever we go.

Seeing others as an addition to our lives means we have to be honest. We have likely been in situations where we have not opened those channels of communication. In order to change, we have to determine that we will change. We must channel that change in ways that allow others to receive a different behavior from what they once saw from us. This can be very freeing. Becoming accepting of others becomes a positive habit, and one that can be developed over a relatively short period of time. When we channel openness, we receive the openness of others.

Churches are such a wonderful place to learn to appreciate different cultures. I remember when one of my nephews married a young lady from India as one of those times. The wedding was beautiful, a combination of traditional Indian wedding ceremonies and a Christian church wedding. I had never attended a wedding reception that combined these two cultures.

I think the parents of the groom had given instructions to the musicians to play traditional Indian music and some very modified American music. They were likely told to limit rhythm and blues music and to stick to some of the classics. We started dancing before the night was over, and I learned that people from India can jam! The channels were open, everyone was receptive, and the folks that were serving us food had to replenish the buffet four or five times. We were having a wonderful time because we were not opposites. Our two families were truly in the moment.

Some of the folks came directly from India, but nothing mattered other than they loved their child, the bride, and we loved our nephew, the groom. Everyone there wanted the day to be a wonderful memory for the newlyweds. Two cultures blended to have a beautiful ceremony, a celebration of a new family. You might want to know if the couple remain married. The answer is yes, and they have two beautiful children. Their union is just one wonderful example of what can happen when we look at people, even those we've never met, as an opportunity.

As we round out this chapter on recognizing people as others, there is one last issue that I do want to bring up, and that is distinctiveness. Others bring distinctiveness that is appreciated. If everyone looked the same, the world would be a place of little distinction. We thrive on differences in our architecture, in our cultures, our ways of worship, and our traditions as countries. We often think that what we do is the only right way, and we discount others when we do so. The ways that others look, speak, dress, and live are a few of the wonderful things that God gives us during our time on earth, and we should be grateful.

We can do so much to enrich our lives with the openness we can channel. We also have to accept that God gives us people whose disabilities we may not understand. At this moment, both of my legs are working. I can walk, but there are others who cannot walk, who may be disabled. Some use wheelchairs, some are blind or deaf and some have disabilities we cannot see, but each of us has his or her distinct life to live and share. We must understand that our abilities can change at any moment, and that we are equally human, regardless of such change. We see people returning from war with physical impairment and the mental anguish that comes with that. We also have those who are with us who have been mentally or physically challenged from birth. Some come to this earth challenged in many ways, but they, too, are distinctive. Our uncomfortableness with these truths can only be faced with an appreciation of all who live on this earth.

Humans share stages in life, from infancy to old age. All stages should be revered, and none should be considered as opposite from our own. Genetics play a role in how we will develop and what we may be on this earth. We must remember that we are all in this together and that God has a plan for each of us. Part of God's plan is that we live together and love one another for who we are on earth. We are shipmates.

## CHAPTER 9 – HOWTO TREASURE THE MOMENTS
**Pipe Down**

In Chapter Eight, we dealt with the idea of opposites and learned how to better appreciate the positive difference that comes with thinking of others as an addition to our lives. We also learned how to channel that positivity to those around us. I consider Chapters Nine and Ten as chapters in which we can relax a bit. We are no longer focusing on specific behaviors but are asked to remember to treasure the moments in life. I think this ability is one of God's most wonderful blessings!

In my attempt to identify ways to treasure the moments, I realize that this first way may not appear to be positive because it begins with the word don't. Standard written English would likely demand that I begin with do not, but if you can tolerate more colloquial usage, you can appreciate my use of don't. Don't take life for granted. If you do, you will fail to treasure many important moments. Don't take life for granted. This is easier to say than do, particularly with today's way of living. Instead, "pipe down," which means quiet down, and savor what is.

I believe that American culture is based on a fix-it ideology. We think we can fix everything in America with one doctor, one pill, one specialist, or one piece of equipment. If my car breaks down, there is someone at the car dealership to fix it. If something is broken in our home, there will be a technician who can deal with the specific repair needed.

But our fix-it mentality isn't very realistic. Again, as we recall Einstein's Theory of Relativity, we know that change comes. Everything and everyone is moving through transition to conclusion. This is a book about that journey. Chapter Nine helps us realize the importance of treasuring the moments of our lives. Chapter Ten deals with developing a plan of action as we move forward, a plan of hope. Part of our growth is to clarify what is meaningful, and to treasure the moments that contain that meaning. We often insist that we don't take life for granted, but the way we live suggests otherwise. If we fail to treasure life's moments, we are speaking one intention but living another.

When you stop taking life for granted, every moment becomes precious. I am blessed to be retired, but I am also apprehensive. Even though I know my mantra of not taking life for granted makes perfect sense, I don't think I have lived by it. Whether you are in your twenties, your fifties, or close to retirement – whatever your stage of life - please don't talk about what you are going to do when you become a certain age or have saved enough money. You need to find ways to make those things happen now, or at least take steps to actualize those goals. Remember, you have no guarantee that you will be here tomorrow! You must treasure the moments while you are living them. When we do that, each meal tastes better, and each contact with others is more pleasant. When you start treasuring the moments, you begin to appreciate getting up each day and spending time with your spouse or significant other.

Seeing children, neighbors, friends and colleagues at work, these times become important if they are valued in the moment they occur. Too often, we find ourselves walking through life with too little appreciation of what each moment holds. Moments we treasure become our gold standard, the diamonds, rubies, and sapphires of life. Let people know you appreciate the moments you have with them often enough, and they will learn to practice what you preach. People learn quickly!

I realize that people have different ways of living their daily lives. I am not saying that everyone is walking around saying they wish they were no longer on this earth, but so many are living as if they have so much hell in their lives. They are projecting so much misery that I have to wonder why they are bothering with life at all. Now, I know that to assume that everything in the world is going to be perfect is not realistic, but we have to deal with the difficulties in life in much the same way as we do the joyful times. Remember, these are the only moments we will get.

Early in this chapter, I introduced the word don't, as in don't take life for granted. Next, I want to reference the word make. Remember, this is a journey book, and I may be journeying into an area that is not so comfortable for me. Make a daily "to be" list. I am not good at making lists but I am task-oriented, which is why I suggest that you make this list on a periodic basis. I believe it would help us go through the day without taking life for granted. The list would make us mindful of treasuring the moments much more than we normally do. What will be on your "to be" list will depend on individual circumstances. While we may fantasize about being taller or more athletic than we are, these aren't the items to put on our list. The list I am talking about is one that focuses on how we impact others. It does not necessarily involve appearance or things we cannot control.

For example, my list would include my intentions to be more open, more caring, and more loving. Also, I would strive to be less irritable and less concerned about other people's business. It would add to the discipline of life, the same discipline that we held ourselves to on the boat. Remember, we have gone through that period. We are off the boat now and must carry on.

You may want to consider some sort of forty-day fast as we move through the annual Lenten season or other holy times of the year. This allows you to be mindful of the sacrifice of Jesus. I remember I gave up carbonated drinks one Lenten season and was going to read one psalm a day for forty days. Giving up the carbonated drinks was not that big a problem, but finding the discipline to read the psalms on a daily basis was tough. You know, it's hard for us to complete tasks if there isn't a carrot, a reward, waiting for us when we finish.

Some of us are more motivated to succeed if we know we will receive some tangible reward. For example, my wife, Gloria, and I never rewarded our children's good grades with financial incentives, although some parents do. When they brought their report cards home, we always asked if they had done their very best. None of the three ever said that they had not done so, and their performance throughout school, college and graduate school was exemplary. The incentive for these three was to graduate, to move from one rung of their education to the next. They were good elementary students, good high school students, good students through college and in graduate school. The incentive was to be good students, which would result in graduation and better lives. If you are in school, making your list of intentions should include being a good student. Success is the reward!

Whatever is said in the next two chapters is applicable to my three focus areas: academics, religion and work. Treasure the moments in each by making that daily list of things to do for yourself in each area in which you spend the days. I believe this will make a great difference in how you treasure each moment.

The next thing I want you to remember is to live in God's daily blessing. There are people who can't get up in the morning or go to sleep at night because they are having trouble in the moments God has given them. If we live in the moments we will treasure them, even those that challenge us more than we think we can bear.

I had jobs in high school that I still treasure. My friend and home boy, Douglas Gaines, always shares the story of one job I had at a toy manufacturing warehouse in Nashville. This was back when it was acceptable to hitchhike. I hitchhiked to work, climbed onto the freeway, jumped over the fence, and walked to my job. Then I would hitchhike home each evening. Just think of that, here I was in the segregated South of the early sixties, hitchhiking rides. Hitchhiking was common then, even though these were years of violence in the lives of African Americans.

So, I had a job at Tip-Top Merchandise, a toy and game warehouse. We had Mattel, Bradley and other toy brands. My job was to fill orders for toys and games, and I was allowed to take the damaged toys and games because they couldn't be sold. I would take the little Matchbox cars to the Southland Bowling Alley where a track was set up for them, and the race was on! Not everybody had a track like this in their bowling alley, something I now realize. So, Douglas and I had those little damaged Matchbox cars racing around that track that I would bring home from Top-Top Merchandise. Now, the white boys would have these fancy little cars of their own, and I'd bring ours in and we would "whip butt" as my home boy would say. We were living in the moment with the blessing of the job and the Mattel Matchbox cars that God had provided me. We started with little cars that were damaged, but we could win because we fixed the wheels so the cars would be fit to race. We would angle a tire, make a repair, whatever it took to put our little cars on equal footing. I don't recall what happened to those little cars, but I do know that my nieces and nephews remember that I often brought them toys from

Tip-Top. I would bring my nephews model planes, and my nieces ended up with all kinds of girl stuff. I was the black Santa from Tip-Top Merchandise.

I really wasn't afraid back then. Hitchhiking was not the safest thing to do, but I was living in the moment and living the blessing of a job that God gave me. I always tell my wife, Gloria, that I try to fear nothing because I live within the blessings that God gives. I've lived in Tennessee, Washington, D.C.; Chicago, Missouri, and Arkansas, and I've always lived without fear in the blessing of what God has given me. I think that fearfulness takes away from the joy of life. We must treasure each moment.

Now that I have discussed don't, I will discuss "do." Do what you can while you can. If there is anything that continues to bother me, it's those times I have not done things while I could. This is a journey book written for all ages by a person in his sixties. I have fewer years in front of me than I have lived. Even so, I am writing this for my two-year-old grandson, the youngest grandchild, and the oldest, my thirteen-year-old grandson. As of this date, I have another grandson who is less than two years old, and my oldest is now seventeen. I write for them as well as my children. I have always told them all to do what they can while they can.

Doing what we can while we can is another way to treasure each moment. Do what you can do while you can, and realize that doing so involves some risk. I have some regrets, as do we all. There are some things I can't re-choreograph, as much as I might like to do so. Einstein's Theory of Relativity has proven that our moments cannot be precisely re-created.

Looking back, I know I would have done some things a little differently. I'm sure I would have made some other choices, perhaps with some risk, because I now realize that I might well have been successful. For example, I could have involved myself in business ventures. There are some cars I should have purchased and others I should have passed on, now that I think about it. Once, my wife and I had an opportunity to buy a home in Tennessee. We didn't take advantage of that, and it might have been a profitable investment opportunity. Our lives demand that we choose. Doing what we can while we can allows us to live in God's blessing, and doing the best we can while we do it shows our thankfulness to Him.

One way to treasure the moments in life is to insist on being treated fairly. You don't have to live a life regretting how you let others treat you, regardless of where you find yourself. We should treat others fairly, and we should insist that we are treated fairly as well. There is a mindfulness to this that relates to the context of this book. Remember, we are all in this together. Nobody jumped off the boat. If we are going to live with one another, we should think of this life in terms of living with ourselves and others. We start by treating ourselves fairly, something we sometimes forget.

When we think of treating ourselves fairly or insisting that others do so, we increase the moments we treasure. This insistence can result in change, however, and change is not always comfortable. Remember Einstein's theory. Nothing remains stagnant. We cannot always meet the expectations of others, nor should we. This brings me to another word I want to introduce. The word is 'no," and it is an acceptable word, an acceptable answer. We need to be able to say no even as we realize that we may be hung out to dry for it. I am reminded of the movie *Crimson Tide* in which the actor Denzel Washington said no to the captain in response to the demand that he launch nuclear weapons. Denzel's character suffers both physically and psychologically for his response to the demand, but he remains steadfast. There had been no clear direction to launch nuclear war, and as is often the case in life, Denzel's character was treated unfairly because others wished to act without fully realizing the implications of moving without a clear message. Simply put, sometimes others order us to move too quickly, and we have to say no in order to live with ourselves. This is something we encounter in every aspect of life. We have to realize that no is an acceptable answer, even if it causes conflict.

We can find ourselves in situations in which people speak quickly or want to act too soon. We have a right to speak up and say no, particularly when there is incomplete information or we feel our integrity is being compromised. It is empowering to say yes or no and to walk through situations in which you, and others, are treated fairly as a result. It is also empowering to wait until we get the necessary information to enable us to make wise decisions. There will be times where that information is not going to be readily available, and it is still within our right to say no. When you understand that dynamic, you can treasure these moments as well.

We all have situations in our lives when it has been hard to hear the truth. When the truth is revealed, however, we must hear it and treasure that moment as well. If we live in that truth, we become one of truth's lights. Living as one of those lights is not always easy. I have made so many mistakes in life that it would take a lifetime to relive them. In order for each of us to treasure the moments, we need to live authentically in lives laden with a truth that comes from the heart. Truth that is hardest for us to accept often demands that we make significant change, another moment to treasure.

The truth continues to do its work on me, and I don't always like it, either. As is the case for doctors and lawyers who are authorized to practice in their fields, we must practice our truth. And in the same way doctors and lawyers approach each case and individual as unique, we must look at one another as unique souls put on this earth to be treasured. We must look at people within their individual situations instead of attempting to categorize them.

To treasure one another means coming to the realization that we have individual standards for what is of value. Our unique lives and experiences have made each of us who we are. In order to treasure the moment we must appreciate what has impacted our lives and how we have responded in each instance. We must also remember that we have to treasure moments for what they were rather than what we wish they had been. That has been most difficult for me, because remember, I, too, am a product of my environment. I am a product of a southern town with southern traditions, but I lived a life that was nontraditional. I went to integrated schools, churches and parks, but I also lived in the black community and experienced the joys and troubles that came with that.

So, I'm a product of all that was Lebanon, Tennessee, but I'm only a product of what I have experienced. I've not experienced enough to be able to look at all people and make stock decisions about them. In essence, I don't know everything. I only know what I know. I continually work on understanding others, and to do so, I have to practice what I preach. I have to meet others where they are rather than where I think they should be. I have to treasure these moments with them in a very profound and loving way, and consider what they could achieve instead of what I think they should do. We should "pipe down," and listen, instead.

## CHAPTER 10 – SUBJECTIVITY
## BLESSED AND CURSE] TOGETHERNESS

This chapter is the prelude to the last in this book. I will be as open with my own views as I can bear. For some, reading this will result in "aha moments." Others may question how I dare communicate such things. The blessing about having been on the boat is that I know that we are all in this together, long after we've left the boat. Another blessing is that God gives us free will, which is a part of what gives us such great joy and agony as we relate to one another. I struggled with this content. Even so, writing this chapter was a cathartic moment for me, an emotional release. We need moments that provide this release, even though they can be challenging.

Also, being off the boat comes with the possibility of expression that might not be so welcome in closer quarters. Both this chapter and the next will be punctuated with bold-faced headings within the chapter to explain a bit about what follows. Some topics are musings, and others are direct comments intended to inform readers of my perception of living in my black skin in a largely white America. All are offered with an open heart and the ability to appreciate others as we all wish to be appreciated.

## THE HUMAN BODY
## HAS AN EXPIRATION DATE

I'll begin with the reality of human physiology. God's plan includes the fact that we share the same physiology, the same bodily functions, regardless of our habitat. Consider blood types. No matter the country of our origin, for example, type O blood has universal characteristics. We all have genetic profiles, and we are also subject to genetic differences or variations, both positive and negative. Although we cannot escape our genetic heredity, we can make the best of what we have been given. If we are genetically programmed to be heavy, we will be heavy, or we will work harder to maintain a trim body. While we may still have the propensity to be heavy, we can affect the outcome. In addition, there is the question of nature or nurture, what we come to this earth with as well as the environmental factors that impact us. I am always amazed about that fact when traveling overseas. We are often told not to drink the water that people who live in the same area consume with no problem. Their bodies have become conditioned to that water, while ours have not had time to do so. We find that travel to places away from home requires that we adapt to different temperatures and even geographic changes that call on us to adapt physiologically. We are fortunate that we can usually do so.

I have mentioned the quick-fix that Americans look to for everything possible, including our bodies. Frankly, our bodies aren't built that way. They are not meant to last forever. We can die from natural causes, or we can develop a terminal condition. Whether we die from natural causes or terminal illness, we will all die. If you think about it, life is a terminal condition. We can treat terminal illness and we can attempt to prolong life through healthful living, but life ends at some point. This isn't a subject we may be comfortable with because death reminds us of our own mortality. Life is part of a cycle, however, and death is the transition from that life.

So, life doesn't last forever, and we can't buy more time here, either. I mentioned in an earlier chapter that my son, Leron, has always said that we have more money than we have time. Many people think they have more time than money, but I disagree. We can't bank on having more time, but we can put money in the bank. We all have a number, something I think of as a holy clock. Christians understand that clock, and we realize that through Jesus Christ, God has given us the hope of resurrection. Non-Christians may have different beliefs as to what happens when we die. I believe that death is something that only Jesus Christ has overcome, and that Christians have eternal life in the hope of resurrection.

While none of us is equipped with a body able to help us avoid the aging process, aging itself is a wonderful thing. Think about it. The older we get, the longer we have lived! And of course, it would follow that our bodies change as we age. Recently, my nephew and I were looking at old college yearbooks and pictures. My mother was to be ninety-seven years old, and we were planning a birthday party for her. As we looked for pictures of her, we saw pictures of ourselves when we were young and dapper. While the Lord has blessed us with additional years, we have aged along the way. We have added a few pounds here, and a few wrinkles there. Body changes and transitions through the stages of life are inevitable. Isn't it a wonderful thing to realize early on that there are no special bodies?  Isn't it good to know that all of us experience aging?

When our time comes, our time comes. This is true in birth and in death, a stark reality, even as we think about all of us being in this together. The fact of our God-given physiology is that we all live and die, something that both humbles and frightens me. We are all in this together, even in death. I grew up with the idea that we all start dying at the age of twelve, something that I heard early on in my home church and within my family. For us, the age of twelve was the beginning of our accountability for who we were, and who we would become. Many of my neighbors and friends grew up with the same tradition, regardless of denomination or whether the exact age of twelve was invoked. So, while I knew I was dying on earth, I was also alive in Christ. I knew I had been living toward my resurrection since baptism.

## ALL COMMENTS ARE NOT MEANT TO ENCOURAGE COMMUNICATION

What is said in speech or put in writing does not always reflect what is being communicated. Unfortunately, what is often said is meant to intimidate, or to show others up. Some people offer compliments in ways that indicate a slight sarcasm or even worse, which is often their intention. The idea of political correctness, for example, has changed from the desire to use language that promotes inclusivity to a notion that any desire to promote inclusivity is somehow less than desirable and even, well, fake. So, communication is a very tricky business, indeed.

I am careful when I consider commentary. I don't usually read the opinions of others, and I am not a big fan of Facebook. I tend to prefer to read something a bit less slanted than the opinions of others. I would rather form my own opinions. Another reason I feel this way is probably a result of my use of commentary as a cited reference in college. I did that one time. My political science professor scolded me so harshly that I've never forgotten it. "Remember a commentary is one person's opinion," he said. I still remember that. I also understand that I am offering either my own opinion, or my interpretation of factual information, as is everyone who communicates.

Many people are not communicating clearly when they respond to a question or to something they have said, read or heard. I listen to talk radio, local and national television stations, and at times, I wonder if I am in another world. The commentator says, "Today we are going to talk about X. Callers, the lines are open." Someone calls in and the commentator says, "Yes, what would you like to add to the conversation?" Rather than answer the question, the caller talks about everything but the question, and seems to have no desire to approach the topic under discussion. Instead, the caller either rambles on without identifying a single topic or promotes his own agenda with no significant connection to the request for a response. I sometimes wonder if these callers fail to understand the question or are simply unable to respond. I think we have to tell folks when they jump off into left field that we appreciate their intention but can't understand why they are talking about something that is not relevant to what was being discussed.

Of course, you can truly treasure some of these moments, too. There are some, for example, who will always answer any question I might ask with information about their little dog, just because they love their little dog. We all know someone like this. The fact that we were talking about the upcoming holiday season or any other topic means nothing to these folks. They just love their little dog or whatever they always come up with, and these people are often people who are among the most precious to us. We can treasure these moments simply because what is important is the time we spend with people. What is said often doesn't matter. These folks have chosen to share some topic that makes them feel safe, comfortable, and happy. There is nothing wrong with pleasant communication, and there is nothing wrong with people who are full of joy and willing to share it.

## TRUTH, AND CURSING, AND POLITICAL CORRECTNESS, OH MY!

How can you treasure the moment when it's hard to hear the truth? Many of us have a hard time hearing the truth. You may recall from an earlier chapter that I mentioned arriving at Philander Smith College in 1965. I spoke of the college's graduation requirements in relation to John 8:32, "Ye shall know the truth, and the truth shall make you free." The truth was that we had to make certain grades to graduate, and no grade less than a C would be accepted. We were younger then, and life was easier. In some ways, I think the depth of truth is harder to hear as we grow older. I have found that hearing the truth can be a time when it becomes difficult to treasure the moment.

I think that many of us just don't want to hear the truth. We may not want to be set free. Think about it. When you are bound by a lie, a falsehood, it puts a line in your mentality. You are bound by it. You don't have to reach past it, you don't have to go out and try to rise above it, and you don't have to hear it. Truth be told, hearing the truth can open up possibilities that we may not want to consider. Once free from mental boundaries, we have choices to make, and making choices can be risky when we are not bound by falsehood and lies that we have continued to allow in our lives. But what wonderful moments can come from that sense of being unbound! These are more moments to treasure. The truth also enables us to be open to the offerings of Christian faith. It allows us to receive what Christ gives us, the opportunity to see the truth through other people who live it, and to see beyond our lies.

I think that our voyeuristic society is enabled by the speed of technology that can now capture every word, facial expression, and casual comment that we make. I believe this also greatly impacts the way we perceive the truth and how we live. There is no one under the sun that is ever one hundred percent truthful, in public or in private. That is not going to stop people from commenting about what we say one way or another, however. I believe what we have to do is be true to ourselves, and that includes being true about what we choose to hear. I'm always amazed by what people say or do, and sometimes I just close up and choose not to hear what is being said. For example, I think that Richard Pryor was one of the greatest comedians there ever was, but I felt that his profanity was unnecessary. I thought his timing, his content, and his ability to communicate with the audience were very entertaining. In my opinion, he didn't add anything to that with cursing.

I have been standing over congregations for thirty-four years. I've made some profane comments too, but not in a public setting behind a pulpit. I think we should remain mindful of where we are, and make comments accordingly. When I was pastoring in Pine Bluff, Arkansas, I was asked to give the opening prayer at a community event. I opened with "As-Salamu Alaikum, Shalom, and God Bless You," greetings of peace to Muslims, Jews, and Christians. I later added that I prayed the prayer in the name of Jesus. After the event, some Muslims in attendance and a Jewish person I knew expressed appreciation for the prayer.

Public prayer that is inclusive can be very well received. If your prayer, your comments, and your conversation with others can be inclusive, you lessen the chance of offending others. If we are all in this together, we all deserve some sense of offering respect and being respected. Those who mock political correctness often forget that inclusivity is vital to a sense of community, which is better for all involved.

The instantaneousness of television coverage has given rise to a new industry of talking heads, people in the media who can discuss any comment for minutes, hours, and sometimes days. The public has a right to know about actions of political figures and others who put themselves in the public eye. This sort of scrutiny is a part of everyday life that is unlikely to change. People are quick to comment about what others say and do because they have nothing else to do, and because the information is so easy to access. Comments made can often be communicated beyond the circle we intend them to be.

That goes back to us all being in this together. Our conversation with one another should be open. Conversation should be something that increases communication instead of shutting it down. It should also be informational and offered in a way that is easy to comprehend. Sometimes that means pacing our communication and fitting it to the person on the other end. I admit that I can be overwhelmed by the younger generation and their communication ways. They know so much more than we did at their age, and I appreciate that. It is important to talk with young people, to listen to them. I talk with my son, Leron, and daughter-in-law, Stacy, about communicating with young people. They are parents now, and both teach. They are artists, too. I asked Stacey once about students using profanity. I can only share my experience when I visited a school, and I say this to ask, where is the dialogue? I would suggest that if your child is in middle-school level or above, you need to take off work and schedule time in the lunchroom when your child isn't there. What you hear may surprise you.

It is hard to hear the message within all the profanity so many young people use. I talked to my daughter-in-law about this She said, "Well, Mr. Mac, for some people, profanity is a way to communicate." My son said the same thing. That's hard to deal with for a lot of us, but profanity is a type of speech. It is their voice, and that voice is often laced with profanity. I believe that for some people, profanity is a vice, an escape mechanism. It can also be used as a shield, a way to push people away, or to attack. Profanity can be used as a way to control, too, to intimidate.

Maybe the most important thing about communicating with young people is that we must listen carefully. I have learned that it is more important that I hear them than it is to focus on how their use of profanity makes me feel. Our youth have something to say, no matter how off-putting their delivery can sound.

I also think about growing up, and who some of us are now. Some of the older folks reading this may have cursed all the time when they were younger. This could be the same with many young people today. Like many of us, their use of profanity will not determine who they are. They will grow up and leave profanity behind. For some it is and was a voice, one way of communicating. There are many ways to communicate, and the use of profanity is one of them. For some it is and was a vice, something they latched onto and used when they wished to be bad.

Regardless of how we label them, words do hurt, and they don't have to be curse words to do that. That old "sticks and stones may break my bones but words will never hurt me," is one of the world's biggest lies. Words don't have to be profane to do damage. If they come from a place of hate or harm, they hurt everyone involved.

## MONEY IS A COMMODITY
## THAT HEAVEN DOESN'T NEED

You can look at it positively or negatively, but money is a commodity to be used. Money that isn't used for good is good for nothing. For example, money that is used to build equity is a valuable resource. I also see some value in buying things that are state-of-the-art. If you do spend a few extra dollars and buy the best you can afford, you often have the advantage of buying a product that is going to last you a little longer than a less expensive item.

We need to use money to help build better lives for our families, our friends, and those around us who need help. The best folks in business understand that money is a commodity. They use money to its best advantage. They understand the dynamics of interest, and compound interest. They know that money saved without interest is likely to lose value through inflation. Money is something that children don't often learn enough about at home. I think basic money management should be taught in our schools. Those in the religious world know that money can be used for fellowship, church enhancements, and benevolence. All are important. We know that money given shall come back to us through blessings bestowed by God. This makes giving perhaps the wisest investment of all.

Christians believe that when we die, we are all going somewhere, be it heaven or hell. In the meantime, we live on earth and believe we should try do our best while we are here. Part of doing our best is understanding that God doesn't need our money. We can serve God, however, by using our money in ways to provide for ourselves and others while we are here. Those who talk about the fact that they don't give to a church or charities are often the first to agree that heaven doesn't need their money.

Since we have agreed that we can't take money to heaven, we should talk about how it can be best used. I hope you notice that I refer to money as being used instead of being spent. Just because we can't take money with us doesn't mean we should flaunt it or throw it away on things that are of little value. Spending money is one thing, and using it is another. I believe that an openness to being truly productive is to understand that money is a commodity, and one that will likely spoil if we don't use productively. Give as God has blessed you so that the more you are blessed, the more you give. Heaven doesn't need money and you can't take it with you, but money can be used for God's will here on earth.

As a commodity, money itself is not the best indicator of prosperity, promise or achievement. When we use money, we should also understand the value it can bring without the idea that what we purchase is always measured by monetary value. I learned this personally through a ministerial assignment in 2006, the year we bought a home in Hot Springs Village, Arkansas. Seven people looked at the house we wanted, and three placed an offer on it. We ended up as the proud owners of the home. When my assignment in Hot Springs ended four years later, I couldn't sell the house for what I paid for it. If I sold it at that point, I would have incurred a forty-percent loss on the property. In the economic recession that occurred during that time, people frequently experienced that kind of loss. Even though we were in a recession, those four years in that house were four of the happiest years of our lives. We lived in a home we thoroughly enjoyed. Just because the market says a home has lost value doesn't mean it has lost value to you. Money can be counted or tracked, but you can't track or count the value of what a home can provide a heart. You can't track mentality, an attitude or what someone is going through. Some things cannot be quantified or measured by money only. Value received from the use of money and the experiences that use brings is something that is gauged by the individual.

Having spoken about the use of money as a commodity rather than something that is just spent, I also want to discuss debt. I believe that debt is detrimental to the majority of Americans, and can result in the re-enslavement of African Americans. Please understand that if there is nothing else that I appreciate in life, I do appreciate "going first class." Most of us enjoy buying quality items that will serve well. I haven't paid cash for everything, but I've always tried to structure debt so that my family was never in a financial bind.

I believe that the consumer behavior of many African Americans puts them in an unfortunate situation where they must make a given amount of money just to survive. This life way often leaves little to be used for moving ahead. When I say that, I'm not talking about the regular eight-hour work day that so many of us perform in this country. I'm talking about the other kinds of work we may have to do to move beyond the survival mode, and how we should structure our use of debt relative to what we earn. Some may be intimidated at the thought of preparing for the kind of work necessary to provide for a life beyond debt. This intimidation can keep us from doing the things for our families that we should do. To succeed often means striving for education. It can also mean leaving our homes to secure employment. It means not satisfying every urge for instant gratification. I also realize that debt is a significant burden for millions of Americans of other races.

I also want to mention that with most of the jobs I have held, I never signed up for overtime. When I worked for the United States Postal Service in the 1980s, there was a young man I knew at work who had a beautiful custom van. I was working part-time then, I got off at six o'clock every evening. The young man and I began to talk on the parking lot one day after work. I noticed that he always appeared to be unhappy, and I finally asked him if there was something wrong. I learned a great deal from him that day. He said, "Man, I don't ever get a chance to enjoy my van. I always have to work overtime, and I need to make that extra money to pay for it." I didn't say anything to him, but I asked myself why anyone would sign up for such a thing. If we worked overtime at the post office, we were always going to work overtime because people were always taking time off. While that may have sounded good to some, the problem I had with it was that he had signed up for overtime and had bought a van that he couldn't afford on his regular salary. I did not see, and still do not see this as a way to move forward. This enslavement of African Americans and others in our nation is a disadvantage that keeps us more concerned about paying on debts owed than improving our lives and those of our children. Those who can't make it on their regular salaries and expand their lifestyles through debt with the addition of supplemental salaries are in jeopardy. They are often susceptible to being taken advantage of by employers who know about their situation.

Having nice things is wonderful, unless we are neglecting our families to sustain those things. Some people have good salaries. They live comfortably on their regular incomes. They can easily afford to purchase what they want, which is often difficult for others who want those things as well. It is important, however, to use money instead of allowing money, in the form of debt, to use us.

My Uncle Johnny always told me, "When you work, you make sure you pay yourself." Every time I got a check, and I don't care if it was just enough to buy a hamburger, I always bought a hamburger. I always made sure I paid myself. When you think about it, that's where some of that psychological push to take on debt affects African Americans and others. We work, and we get paid. And at the end of the day, we still may not have enough to pay what we owe. This is a bind that many find themselves in, and it can seem insurmountable. Our lives can be in shambles because of debt, with creditors hounding us for money we don't have. At one point in my life, I wasn't making enough income. The debts were overtaking me, and I did what so many others should do. I contacted every single creditor I had and asked to pay a progressive amount toward the full payment of each debt. As uncomfortable as being in too much debt is, everyone can make steps to get themselves on the right financial road. I encourage anyone in this situation to talk to your creditors before you get even deeper in debt. Contact them and see if you can negotiate a payment plan without the interest rate continuing to grow on a balance that will never decline until you do so. I've been blessed to have pretty decent jobs most of my life, and I wasn't going to let a job enslave me. My family and I made sacrifices so I could go to college, and I also saw to it that my children went. Education is still the best investment for future earning power.

I approached every job I had fifteen years before I got into the ministry with the attitude that I went there looking for a job, and I would leave there looking for one. I was not going to be enslaved to the point that an employer would think that I couldn't make a living elsewhere. As I moved into the United Methodist ministry, I learned that once ordained as a United Methodist pastor, I would go where the Bishop sent me. I did so for thirty-four years. I went where the Bishop sent me, and I gave my full attention to each assignment.

While this may be a bit off topic, I must profess that I think African-Americans have too many part-time churches with part-time pastors. Remember, if you are paying the pastor for part-time service, you may be getting a part-time ministry. You may have the pastor's full attention on Sunday, but pastoring is done during the week, too. Personally, I want to be pastored by someone who is available seven days a week, twenty-four hours a day. While this doesn't directly relate to African Americans and consumerism, it does draw attention to how much time we seek from our spiritual leaders. Perhaps we are comfortable with part-time spirituality so we can spend the rest of the time on more worldly pursuits.

## THE POLITICS OF PROMOTION

The best qualified people don't always get promoted. This is the absolute truth. It is also something to remember when you are the person best qualified for a promotion that is given to someone else. Notice that I say "when" rather than "if." If you believe that the reason you didn't get the job is because of discrimination, go to the Equal Employment Opportunity Commission, or file a lawsuit. You have a right to do so. Regardless of whether or not discrimination has occurred, however, the best person is not always promoted. When that happens and you are the best person, don't get an attitude. Instead, get a clear understanding that you will be able to overcome what has occurred. Being passed over can become much like a mental dagger. When I think of daggers, I think of how they are put in people's backs, figuratively or literally. They often impact people's minds, too. This feeling can happen in any work situation, and we can be "stabbed in the back" without ever knowing it.

When I worked at the post office, the politics of promotion involved getting an easier mail carrier route. The postal service jobs are assigned on a seniority basis. You always start your employment there at the bottom of the ladder. When I started working there, I had what you call a billy goat route, a route that had a lot of hills. Nobody wanted it, so they always put the newest man on that route. I guess they wanted to see if you really wanted to remain with the post office. I think I carried that route a year or two, but to make a long story short, I wanted to get a better route. So, I was bidding on a better one, but the politics of promotion came to bear. The fellows in the union - there were no women carriers at that time - were telling me things about the route I wanted. They said that another man was going to bid on it. I knew that the man in question had more seniority than I did. I ended up not bidding on the job because of that. When the route sheet came out, somebody with lower seniority than I had got the route I wanted.

That's the politics of promotion. I worked in a union structure and assumed that I was protected within that. I was just stupid, and I don't like to use that word. But it was just stupid of me not to bid on that job.

When you think there is an opportunity for you, there is only one way to deal with the politics of promotion. Bid, ask, and inquire. If you have to apply, go on and apply. Don't determine that you won't apply because somebody else is better qualified or has more time and grade than you. I think we used the same terms in the post office as in the military. We talked in terms of time and grade. In the military, you just couldn't be an E-5 sergeant one day and get promoted to E-6. If another E-5 sergeant had been a sergeant for four years or more, that sergeant was promoted first. But the politics of promotion is one of those things I threw in there because it is coming from getting a bigger basket, tying us all together again. However, the politics of promotion is also a thing of beauty. What happens at work can dramatically change our life way. Who knows what would have happened if I had gotten that route I once wanted.

God works in God's way all the time, and He does that for us. For those from the philosophic perspective, it works the same for you as for Christians. Your faith or non-faith base will not spare you from life's politics. Prayer or no prayer, it makes no difference. I had a friend who was very Pentecostal, and he was going up for a test, a supervisory test, for a better position. He knew God would help him answer those questions, and he didn't do any studying. And he received a grade that reflected his lack of studying, too. The next time he studied for about a year, and he passed the test. You have to prepare yourself. There are politics in promotion when you are prepared as well politics when you are not prepared. Either way, you have to prepare.

## NETWORKING—NOT WHAT WE GET BUT WHAT WE GIVE

For me, networking is neither racial nor generational. Networking means that we are all in this together, and at our best, we can communicate to improve the lot of one another.  One of the things I have found is that we have different social, economic, and political layers in America. Networking is found within each layer, although some prefer that others might not move as freely among the layers as they do.  We must understand networking is about what we can give as well as what we might receive. Networking enables us to grow and allows us to thrive within the realm of education, in business, and within our church and local communities. I don't think we take into full account the value of networking. We literally need to widen our net so that we can advance our connections. To do so means we have to understand that to network successfully, we have to be available.

Find out those places you need to be, place yourself there, and get things done.  As I think about, we have not done enough in the academic area to broaden the scope of education, because education  today often appears to end with a period. You may recall that I talked about commas and periods earlier.  I think we are trying to educate our students for this moment, for such a moment as this.  We want you to learn this, period. I think this is an educational trap, one in which we are binding our students. I think there should be more networking, even among the most practiced educators and school administrators.  Teachers, parents, and educators who understand that teachers need more time to network with one another could greatly benefit by giving teachers that time.  They would also benefit by paying teachers well for the additional time they spend doing their best to teach our children. We pay for what we value, and surely we find more value in the hours our children spend with teachers than is evident in the low salaries we pay them.

I strive to enable young folks to be learners now and throughout their lives.  I don't think I missed many days in all the years I was in school, from the time I was a five-year-old at Leeman's Corner School to the time I did post master's degree work. In my almost nineteen years of education, I probably missed school one or two times, and that's the truth. I loved school, and it wasn't all about the learning. Sometimes it was about the girls being there, the sports I played, the plays I was in, or just being there and seeing friends.

I guess school led me to the career path that I continued through the years. I hope I have been one of those who enjoys people wherever they are, regardless of their socioeconomic status. If I go somewhere and people are Ripple and they want me to have a drink, I will have a drink with them. If I'm in an exclusive community and somebody offers wine or aged whiskey, I will have a drink of that as well. Socializing is another way of networking, and it is also part of enjoying others and being comfortable with yourself. The same holds true as we move in others areas that are going to be productive for us and to which we can contribute. We have to broaden our scope and network with folks who are outside our immediate circle. These times widen our opportunity and we benefit from less isolation.

Remember that we are all in this together, and we have to learn how to deal with those different from ourselves. We can benefit from the network that results. I have tried my best to live what I preach in this regard. It is not enough to broaden our circle just to derive benefit. When we give, we have the opportunity to be part of the greater structure, and we make a positive difference.


## AN INTERNATIONAL UNDERSTANDING

I don't have any translators at the moment, but I do think I would like to see this book translated in as many languages as possible. America is becoming more diverse, and for many of us, English is not our first language. No matter what language or languages we speak, we are all in this together. We also know that in this world, people can be very easily manipulated, and that there will always be some level of conflict within each country, and among nations. Some people will prosper more than others, at least here on earth. Others less prosperous will be working every single day just to try to feed their children and maintain a decent place to live.

We have a world history of those who gain power and often fail to consider the good of the people they impact. Many have no regard for anything other than what they can gain for themselves on the backs of those they rule, while other countries try diplomatic approaches to improve life for all. Nonetheless, we all have an international understanding of our world, at least to some extent. We also see our world becoming much smaller, a result of our ability to travel, both nationally and internationally, and to search the internet. We are becoming closer and closer to one another, in both a physical and an electronic sense.

We struggle with the human relations aspect of this closeness. America was built on immigration, but it has become a challenge for us. With all the political posturing that would suggest otherwise, people have been making money from immigrant labor for as long as immigration has occurred. The capture and relocation of Africans who were enslaved built this country, as did immigrants who built railroads and other infrastructure that paved the way for economic development. Many continue to benefit from the growth and expansion of crops, and the financial wealth for which slave labor was responsible. Generations of African Americans continue to impact America through their culture, their talents, and their participation in the American economy, all a result of the sin and shame of slavery.

There are many layers within the immigrant story. There are those who come to this country legally and have documentation, as well as those who enter illegally. While both sets have prospered and also become vital contributors to American society, both have been misused and abused by this country. Illegal immigrants have filled the pockets of those Americans who hired them to build their own considerable wealth, even as they lament the idea that these same immigrants bring needs for services along with them when they arrive. Immigrants often come with little preparation. Illegal immigrants arrive with no voice because they have no citizenship. To fully appreciate the aspects of immigration, both legal and illegal, we must understand the dynamics of this struggle as well as the fact that we are all in this together. Immigrants have almost always contributed much more to American than they are given, and the vast majority come to this country fully willing and expecting to do so.

The debate surrounding immigration will always be with us. In America and around the globe, immigration affects everyone involved. Both Britain and America have seen recent political upheaval as the majorities in each country have come to fear and resent those that come to their borders. Fears of immigrants taking jobs are often unfounded. Immigrants often perform jobs that those in their new countries are unwilling to do.

As countries become more diverse, many fear the inevitable reality that Caucasians will cease to be the majority. Classism includes a sense that those who come to America are of a lower class than those who have generations of American citizenship. This ideology has been evident since America was founded, even as we understand that we are all in this together. I predict there will always be immigration, and that systems will have to be adjusted to allow for who comes, and when. I also believe that our physiology remains the same as human beings, and that we must also broaden our understanding of

101

what all of us being in this together means. America has been a country that has led the free world because of its willingness to interject itself and influence global issues. The election of 2016 has shone light on a conservative, more closed nativism that indicates that many of us are no longer content to celebrate our own people, and to share in global responsibility and leadership. There is strength in that global responsibility and willingness to lead that I fear we will lose as a result.

When we consider the global perspective, we must realize that as we go through life on this earth, we shouldn't live with an "us versus them" mentality, particularly as we consider educating children and living our day-to-day lives. We have global standards that are shared educationally, for example. What constitutes two of anything is two, regardless of the language or symbol that is used to describe that two. Music is music, and notes that make up that music are shared internationally. The only difference is in the social sciences, our most significant barrier because each country hosts different political and social structures.

Internationally, America is referred to as a Christian country. According to the 2012 review by the National Council of Churches, there are over 68 million Catholics in America. As Hispanic numbers increase, it would be safe to say that overall Catholic members in the United States will continue to grow. The Southern Baptist Convention has over 16 million members, and the United Methodist Church has a membership of almost 7 million. The Church of Jesus Christ of Latter-day Saints has over 6 million members, and the Church of God in Christ has over fifty-five million. A 2015 study estimates that 450,000 Christian believers in this country come from a Muslim background, and most belong to some form of Protestantism. America's diversity will continue to impact church membership, as will the need for religious leaders with the understanding it takes to serve these members.

American business, religion and education will continue to be impacted internationally, by those from without and those within. Those who arrive here from without will give birth to children who will become contributing citizens of this country. They will be engaged in education, business and religion. In order to continue to have a place internationally, Americans must broaden their scope and expand their international concept of understanding and appreciation. Only then will we continue to lead the rest of the free world.

## CHAPTER 11 – KNOW YOU ARE LOVED

Know you are loved. Of all that I have said, please remember this. I fear that America has discounted love to the point that we have truly forgotten the essence of it. For those who are Christians, I am talking about the kind of love our Lord and Savior gave us. For those who are not Christians, I speculate that for you, love comes from heart to heart. The epitome and the essence of love in the Christian faith is what we call agape, or self-giving love. Whatever the perspective, Christian or non-Christian, we must realize that we are worthy of love and that we are loved in order to treasure the moment and to love others.

When you know that you are loved, you are able to live in peace. And peace is unpredictable. It is not something easily defined. One person might find peace in the midst of a noisy NASCAR race, a gym, or a bustling department store, while for others, peace could be a sedentary experience such as that we have when we are in that wonderful place of being half-awake or half-asleep, depending on how we view that state. Peace is different for each of us. But to truly treasure the moment, we must understand that we are loved to enjoy peace that comes with a sense of self-worth that begins to develop from birth.

What I see today is what I believe to be a lack of love. It is causing some of the violent behavior we see in the world, and it is something to which people may, unfortunately, become conditioned. This topic may make some of us feel uncomfortable, but the way my parents disciplined me would be considered child abuse today. Many find themselves in the same position, and we tended to discipline our children in the same fashion. I'm just looking at my hands now and thinking about that. I don't think my mother ever let my father use a switch as big as my thumbs to whip me, but she did let him get one as big as my fingers. This also brings to mind my old football days and how the coaches laid hands on us. I don't think I remember any coach kicking me, but I do know that I was a scrub. I was fourth string in 1959, so I didn't even have a face mask. Once I was big enough to get a face mask, I was jerked around by that mask in ways that were clearly meant to get my attention. In the military in the late 1960s, drill sergeants still put their hands on the men.

I say all that to say that times have changed. Times have changed, indeed. And that is a good thing. When it comes to physical discipline, the fact that we do things differently now is for the better. Regardless of how my parents and so many others disciplined their children fifty or sixty years ago, most of us agree that they did something right because we turned out well. I do know that they loved me, and they dealt with me the only way they knew. And I also know that that which you know in your heart becomes a reality in your life.

I will move from 1948 to today so that I can talk about how knowing you are loved allows you to live in peace. I have already acknowledged that each of us finds peace in our own way. I may not find it where you do. Also, if you don't have a place where you can find that peace, you need to find one. If you don't have that place, you are unable to actualize any love given to you. When you think about people all on that boat together, and about being there for an unknown amount of time, everyone had to find a way to live in peace, to treasure the moments.

We must also consider the phenomenon of violence, both in our country and worldwide. There's an American phenomenon of outright meanness toward others, and it scares me to think of what will become of us. I know that violence is a part of many subcultures as well, a way to strike out at others from a sense of anger and frustration. Unfortunately, violence is evil, regardless of why it is employed, And in certain situations, violence is how people control others. Please remember that violence is not always physical. There was no need to continue to shackle many African Americans. Even without the placement of physical restraints, their minds continued to be shackled.

The way you shackle a person's mind is by placing them in a situation where they have no peace. Someone in school without peace has little ability to learn. Someone in a church where they find no peace will receive little spiritual fulfillment. A person at work with no peace cannot fully perform. Therefore, we must know that we are loved to live in a state of peace, and we must live in that state of peace to move forward. Closed minds, spirits, and hearts rob us of the ability to treasurer the moments in love of one another as human beings. When we are open to others, we experience the peace that comes from treasuring the both the moments and the people who are part of each and every single moment we treasure.

There are some in America who isolate themselves from others. They will talk a good game about how open they are, but if you look at their life style, they are isolated. They are isolated on their job, in their churches, and in their environment in terms of where they live. They are isolated in their social clubs, their communities, their churches and businesses. They can say they are open, but they appear open to only those in their immediate circle.

In order to treasure the moment, we have to cope with some uncomfortable situations. We all have our likes and dislikes. We each prefer favorite foods, different types of weather, and homes and clothes that we find attractive. We all prefer what we want and often fail to be open to anything new or different. If we aren't open to others, we will remain isolated. This is true for both Christians and non-Christians. If they read the Bible, they will learn of these times in the Bible from Genesis to Revelation. All the characters in the Bible had times when they were not open to others. When that happened, God had to step in.

Look at poor Job's situation. He was going through trauma, and when his three best friends came in, he was open to none of them. As a matter of fact, Job also refused to be open to God. For many chapters in Job, you read his struggle with God until Job 19:25. He says, "I know that my Redeemer liveth and that at the last He will stand up on the earth."

Then we look at Moses. Talk about someone who was not open to others! He got to a point of absolutely impunity. He murdered someone. There is a bona fide murderer in the Bible. And this is the paradox for many Christians who get upset with people who have done such wrong. They want to write people off as a result of what they have done.

Moses certainly was not open to the Egyptians. We must treasure the moment even in the midst of tragedy such as this. We can still use tragedy as a back drop, a challenge to uplift. Seeing it might inspire us to realize that there are people in our own communities who have done heinous things. Many of us have done heinous things, and murder isn't the only example. We need to reach out and say to others, let me have a time that I can treasure, some time with you while God is with us. At one point, we have to ask what we can learn from this.

In the Holy Bible, there is the story of Esther. Esther 4:14 is one of the most powerful passages for me. "For if you keep silent at such a time as this, release and deliverance will rise for the Jews from another quarter, but you and your father's family will perish. Who knows? Perhaps you have come to royal dignity for just such a time as this." In order for us to treasure the moments, we have to know "for such a time as this." It might be the time that you speak up for a disabled person, a person of another race or ethnicity, for yourself or someone else, or for someone who cannot bear the burden that is on them. For such a time as this might be an opportunity for you to be open to others. And when you look at the world in such a way that others

108

are part of who you are, it makes a profound difference in the way you live.

When we think about it, to treasure the moment and to know that we are loved gives us the chance to support others. So many behave as if they feel unloved. Maybe they can't feel the love of Jesus or can't know its impact. They can't understand Godly love or even understand why people do what they do. To know that we are loved enables us to give support to others.

## GET A BIGGER BASKET

I have always tried to encourage my children and others to get a bigger basket. Folks don't always know what this means, so going around and telling them to get a bigger basket requires some explanation. I am talking about the steady flow of blessings God gives us, and how some of us are still being blessed from the same baskets we had when we were teenagers. We wonder why our blessings aren't getting any bigger when we should be getting a bigger basket. You see, God can fill the biggest basket that we can find.

As many Christians know, Proverbs 3:4-10, Deuteronomy 14:24-36, and 2 Corinthians 8:13-15 contain some of the same stories found in Matthew, Mark and Luke. You won't find this story in the book of John because that book is a separate Gospel with a decidedly different message. You can find it in the synoptic Gospels of Matthew, Mark and Luke, as the three books contain similar stories.

### Luke 5:1-11
**1** So it was, as the multitude pressed about Him to hear the word of God, that He stood by the Lake of the Gennesaret, **2** and saw two boats standing by the lake; but the fishermen had gone from them and were washing their nets. **3** Then He got into one of the boats, which was Simon's, and asked

him to put out a little from the land. And He sat down and taught the multitudes from the boat. **4** When He had stopped speaking, He said to Simon, "Launch out into the deep and let down your nets for a catch." **5** But Simon answered and said to Him, "Master, we have toiled all night and caught nothing; nevertheless at Your word, I will let down the net. **6** And when they had done this, they caught a great number of fish, and their net was breaking. **7** So they signaled to their partners in the other boat to come and help them. And they came and filled both the boats, so that they began to sink. **8** When Simon Peter saw it, he fell down at Jesus' knees saying, "Depart from me, for I am a sinful man, O Lord!" **9** For he and all who were with him were astonished at the catch of fish they had taken **10** and so also were James and John, the sons of Zebedee, who were partners with Simon. And Jesus said to Simon, "Do not be afraid. From now on, you will catch men." **11** So when they brought their boats to land, they forsook all and followed Him.

This particular verse is a story about folks who had been trying to catch fish. They had been unsuccessful. When Jesus tells them to go back out and cast their nets again, they do so, and they start catching fish. Here is where the blessing comes in, not only for us but also for others. Not only did the men go back out and catch fish; they caught so many that they couldn't keep them all for themselves, and other men came along and began to fish as well.

We are all in this together, and this togetherness continues to go around and around. When I relate the story of Simon to the idea of getting a bigger basket, I share that fact that not only has God been blessing us, but it blesses us to keep a bigger basket. Because of that, my basket overflows and I can help someone else.

Charity begins at home and spreads abroad. I pray that I have given enough charity at home, and I want to give to the church and the community as well. We should give financially and through our whole life way. The concept of getting a bigger basket is a Godly way of looking at life. When you get a bigger basket, you can allow your dreams to grow in number and size. Maybe you played junior high school basketball. Then you continued to high school and played basketball there, too. Each time, your dreams got bigger and bigger, and Gods filled your basket. And never forget the little baskets He filled for you earlier in life. This is a truth across generations and should be shared by elders with the young. The idea that we can grow dreams and that God will fill them to overflowing provides a positive outlook for the young, and a way to sustain ourselves through appreciation of what we have as we grow older.

We should remember those who helped us as we achieve diplomas, certificates, degrees, and other credentials, awards and accomplishments. We have all benefitted from the help of others and should never forget our families, the sacrifices they made, and the push they provided. Our favorite teachers, the high school principal, and all the other persons involved in our school years should never be forgotten. They gave us more than we can ever return, and they often gave of themselves to do so in ways that we will never know.

As a pastoral supervisor, I was expected to supervise people with whom I had attended school. This was not easy, as we had all started school together. We all understand this situation, too. We start work and some of us get to a certain point and the next thing we know, someone else is promoted and we become angry. We talk about it as long as four or five of us can, drink some beer and talk about it after work. When somebody else gets a promotion, the rest of us want to throw them out of our little club. The whole concept of getting a bigger basket includes the fact that we should never forget the friends and others with us as we were moving ahead. If we remember those people, we are much more likely to be in a situation in which everyone can be affirmed and can support each one's successes.

## JUST SAY HELLO

Just saying hello can be such an easy, pleasant thing. Anything more than that can be an issue. I remember a day when I had taken a friend of mine to the doctor. It was a cool day but the sun was shining. I left the parking area and walked across the street, which meant I had moved from the sunny side of the street into the shade. There was someone coming down the sidewalk, and as we met, I made a casual remark that I should have stayed on the other side of the street because it was "sunny over there." And the response from the person was, "You know it's winter, don't you?" Anyway, I couldn't say a word. I had offered a casual, pleasant comment with a smile, all meant to be taken as a greeting, and what I received wasn't at all what I expected! There was a receptionist in the office that I reached within another minute. I simply said hello as I entered, and she responded with the same. As a matter of fact, we had a nice conversation. Then I went on down to the floor where my friend was. This situation really said something to me about how to treasure the moment.

There will be some people in life that we will meet only one time, one time in our entire lives. So rather than saying something catty or saying something about what you see or what you hear, just say hello. When you speak to a person you know, just say hello. There are some people who aren't quite ready for the early morning chitchat that you might enjoy. They just aren't quite ready to engage in conversation.

Believe me I take full responsibility for that conversation on the street that day. I would have felt better if I had just said hello and may have gotten a better response. But that may be wishful thinking too. It was not only the tone of what the person I spoke to had said that impacted me, it was also my reaction. Now this is not a perfect book and I'm not coming at it like I'm hitting all the right notes. There are also people you may see every day that you should still only say hello to, at least for starters. You don't know what mood they might be in that day. We don't know what others have experienced since we last saw them or what their mood may be. So, beginning with "Oh, isn't it a nice day and so and so and so" may not be our best approach. The best thing to do is simply say hello, good morning or how are you, and then move on. The ability to treasure the moment often lies in the ability to condition ourselves to the realization that others may well react to things differently from the way we do. As a matter of fact, we should expect that. We are not always going to say the right thing, and we may often enter a conversation in the wrong place and at the wrong time. It is much better to use common courtesy instead of trying to be clever or overly familiar in many situations.

Eight years of being in a supervisory role, twenty-six years of dealing with all kinds of personalities in the local church, and then fifteen years of working in the government has taught me something. Whether I was on my postal route or whether I was up in east Tennessee at the steam plant working with the Tennessee Valley Authority, I learned that there are many people in the world who are very appreciative of two things: a simple hello and you moving on and getting the hell out of their way. They don't want to talk to you and they don't much care about what you have to say. It's taken me many years to be able to appreciate people like that, but I am much closer to that point now. There are many people that I can just say hello to and move on. They don't have to tell me how they are feeling, and I don't have to ask. Based on the whole concept of the "balancing piece in our lives" that one of my sons is always talking about, we are going to have those days. I don't know where the scale is with each person, but it might be up or down at any given moment. And for some, the scale falls heavily on either side, which is also impossible to predict. So, treasure the moment, just say hello, and move on.


## CUSSING IN A CADILLAC


It was hot and we were in downtown Atlanta, by Georgia State University, in 2013 or 2014. My son and I were riding along and noticed an African American woman in a new model Cadillac. She caught our attention because she was cussing so loud that you could hear her for four or five blocks down the street. She wasn't using every day, four-letter cuss words, either. The bulk of what she said consisted of GDs, MFs, and SOBs, and she included words that painted a great deal of biological imagery about where somebody needed to go and what they should do when they got where she told them to go . . . and it just hurt me.

I think African Americans, particularly if we have been blessed with a good life, need to refrain from such language. God has allowed us to arrive at a certain place, and not all of us are there yet. Because some of us have not always had nice things, you hear that argument on the other side as well. Others of us haven't achieved having nice things to this day. I'll refer back to the Scriptures as I consider this. I am trying to do all I can to help folks out of that situation, to better themselves, to live more comfortably, and to find a better way. It helps us all to know that we are in this together.

I'm not saying that prosperity should cause us to refrain from cursing. I do think, however, that if that woman had been in a vehicle that didn't cost as much as a new Cadillac, it may not have bothered me as much. Beneath my burden as an African American is a cultural obsession. I don't know if I have talked about the obsession of who we, African Americans, are in this country. I wrote about this in one of my seminary papers, and I don't think my professor understood a great deal of what I was trying to say. You see, I have a cultural obsession that moves me to hope and strive wherever I find myself. I don't have a culture obsession that compels me to own a certain house, drive a certain kind of car, or achieve a certain type of degree. There is a historical cultural obsession in me, however, that lets me know that I come from a culture in which people died so that I could be here. My obsession comes from the cultural link between Africa and America, and my culture's historical progression from the motherland. I can hear the voices of those crying out from the Atlantic Ocean, from the millions of Africans who died mid-passage, some due to disease, harsh conditions, or physical abuse. God only knows what they endured. How they were treated in no way reflected who they had been before they were enslaved. They could have been kings or queens before they were sold into slavery, and then separated from their families as if they never existed as families before that point. And I can still hear the voice of Emmett Till crying from the water, a fourteen-year-old African American child who was lynched in 1955, in Mississippi, for reportedly flirting with a white woman.

I still feel that historical cultural obsession because African American children grow up within a social norm that we have adopted. I don't normally curse, but I do know all the words. I'm sure I have said them and am still capable of saying them now, if need be. Just thinking of the public display of this woman and the profanity she was using was totally disheartening to me. I could almost feel the pain that her ancestors might well feel. Her behavior was so disrespectful to them, and to herself. I believe that they would surely not want their descendant to be displayed in public, dishonoring their family through the use of such language. It's not so much about cussing in a Cadillac because it could have been a Lincoln or Mercedes or some other model. It was just the idea that she would behave that

115

way when so many had worked so long to arrive at a place where life is good. We don't want any of our own to belittle what we have achieved through vulgar language and disrespectful behavior.

The other part of the situation is that the woman in the Cadillac was moving. She was driving along with the window down. So, that means that I couldn't know how long her tirade had lasted, and she may have done the same thing at the next stop light. But we are all in this together, and I am embarrassed that other people heard her. Even though I realize that some of my Caucasian friends may or may not understand the dynamics of my historical cultural obsession as an African American, it is likely to be similar to their interest in their own heritage, their genealogy. All of these things can be tied to the way people look at others and themselves.

There is a historic cultural obsession within many African Americans. These are those of us who understand the dynamics of trying to reach a certain mindset and life way that our parents, grandparents and great-grandparents can look on with pride. I am hoping and praying that my children will think enough of their mommy and daddy to continue to do the good things they are doing. I think they are the best three children in the United States of America and the whole world! I believe their spirit has rubbed off on their own children, their friends, and others around them.

I also believe that folks are not going to stop cussing in their cars, or while they are walking. Folks will keep on cussing, and God will keep on blessing.

## DEVELOPING A HOPE PLAN

I really struggle with using the word "plan" because it can be somewhat restrictive. However, I am referring to a "hope" plan. I know that many of us have not lived a life of guidance. I think I spoke earlier about the happenstance of my life. There wasn't a great deal of actual planning because there wasn't a great deal of guidance, although I did receive a great deal of Holy guidance. And I will be grateful for that Holy guidance forever.

I think I have done a little better with my children. There was not so much direct guidance, but we did provide a great deal of indirect guidance through our actions. Our children saw within my wife and me the bigger lessons of life. They learned the importance of becoming educated and providing a secure family life. We showed them through our behavior how to be responsible as mothers and fathers, and the importance of gainful employment. We provided spiritual guidance as well. I have told my children that I struggled to guide them because they have very marketable talents that I think I could have pushed a bit, had I instilled in them an entrepreneurial mindset.

This guide covers education for financial stability, for our life way. I won't mention the communities where I have lived because to me, the assessment varies. If you say "It's a good community," someone else could say, "You mean the one that was on the news where the people there were having so many problems?" People are having problems everywhere, in every community. This is something to think about. We've been blessed in the house that we live in now. We've had this house for over twenty years. It's in a predominantly African-American community. We feel comfortable here. I'm not saying we keep the doors unlocked. I grew up in that kind of environment though. When I left Little Rock and went home to Tennessee, I would continue to lock my car doors and the doors at my mother's and sister's house. When they asked why I was locking the doors, I would say "Well, don't you lock them?" And they replied, "If somebody wants something they can come in and get it." Then I thought back to the times when I was a kid, when my buddy, Roger, and I would go outside and play. Roger's grandmother lived right down the street. And if we wanted something and nobody was at home, we would just go in the kitchen and get whatever we wanted. We had direct - and indirect - guidance.

Of course, direct guidance has its pros and cons. I think that some children, if guided to go west will deliberately go east. I am a child of the sixties, and I don't know how many will relate to my experience. I think our parents were guided by God as far as their faith led them. But when it was time for me to go to college, they just turned me loose. Lord knows I had never been to Arkansas in my whole life. My parents didn't know what was going to happen. They knew folks who had been to college, but they never went. They didn't know what was going to happen once I got there, and they didn't spend time finding out, either. Many of the children of the sixties were like that. My mother did say to me, and I never will forget it, that I was "living off the prayers of others."

I came to Arkansas and was blessed to be associated with a family who understood the dynamics of owning land, something that had a significant impact on me. I learned the value of owning property. Most of my in-laws owned property and have maintained it to this day. I believe that experience provided indirect guidance to my two married sons. They also have property. My daughter and her husband have property as well. I never told them to get a house when they married. I did not tell them to further their education when they finished high school. I believe there was some indirect guidance there as well. They were indirectly guided by example, and it worked. I believe in a hope plan and, I think it is the only way for a worldwide community to understand that we are all in this together.

There is no one thing that we can do to make life a great deal better for some people. Their situations and circumstances may not improve no matter what we aspire to do for them. What we can do is not make their situations worse. However, we can do some environmental things about how we relate to one another. There is a subculture of those who "do not have" that we can improve, almost one person at a time. At my mother's ninety-seventh birthday, my nephew said, "I have been bad all my life. I have been good for the last three months, for the first time in my life." Hear what I'm saying. He's twenty-years old and he knows he's been bad all those years, but we aren't putting him out of the family. He was in the subculture, and has also been in jail. I never saw him smoke dope, but he may have done that, too. His uncle, his grandmother, and his mother didn't give up on him then, and they aren't going to give up on him now. Hopefully, he won't relapse. We, his family, are doing all we can to provide direct guidance. When he was in trouble ten or so years ago, I would write letters for my sister. I would call the Department of Correction in Nashville, Tennessee, too. I was trying to be a good uncle, and to help.

Family troubles are difficult. Sometimes we think that when we go through so much for those who are in trouble that they will go along with our plans for improvement, but that's not going to work all the time. They can see your guiding light sometimes, though. They may not like the plan you write down, but they can see a guiding light because they can see how you are letting your own light shine. "This little light of mine, I'm gonna let it shine." Don't let me preach. I will do so at the drop of a hat.

This hope plan is really an understanding of the importance of guidance. I will end this by saying that God has guided me to this place, and I hope in this guidance that you will find some direction and offer it to others in need. That is the greatest blessing guidance could possibly give.

## ONE HUNDRED OR ZERO PERCENT IS NOT REALISTIC

I firmly believe that nothing about life is at one hundred percent, and nothing is at zero percent, either. I have mentioned Einstein's Theory of Relativity several times, and continue to relate it to the fact that nothing can be fully re-created exactly as it was.

I have heard many wonderful speakers talk about people's lives, and even they want to talk about people's lives as based on one extreme or another. No one's life is absolutely perfect, and neither is anyone's life absolutely miserable. I do think we can become so used to thinking in extremes that we see ourselves at either zero or one hundred percent, with nothing in between. I also think we follow this pattern because of what others say or where we place ourselves.

I've known church members and others who have been very dogmatic about the Scriptures and The Ten Commandments. They often say that all we have to do is live by the Ten Commandments one hundred percent of the time. That may or may not be a good reference for all of us. Regardless of your religious status, however, you are not going to honor anyone by living at one extreme or the other. There is always space between one hundred and zero percent, and we live our lives within that space.

## THE TEN SECOND STEP-BACK RULE

This all came about one day when I went to take my friend for his physical rehabilitation appointment. I had been taking him for six weeks. Every Thursday I would drive up to the facility, open the door, and go in to get a wheelchair. And on the sixth week it happened. A lady came out and she said, "Are you going to park there?" That just struck me the wrong way. I'd been doing this for six weeks, and it looked like she would have known what I was doing and why.

Luckily, I later realized that this is where the ten second step-back rule should have come to play. The lady was dressed in business attire and was not the regular attendant. That should have gotten my attention. In hindsight, she was likely from the office. But rather than stepping back and trying to analyze what was going on, I went on this tirade. "Madam," I said, "I have been doing this for six weeks. I have been bringing him up here, and I am going in like this." She said, "I'm not trying to give you a hard time." If I saw the lady again, she would probably look at me and say that I'm the man who gave her a hard time. She might also add that all she did was ask me if I was going to park there.

The whole thing about the ten second step-back rule is that the need for it can happen so fast that we don't realize it. We can be in a good mood, and boom, something happens. I don't know what the psychologists call it, but there are some indicators here. Number one, when I pulled up, I did not see the regular attendants. There were three or four of them, and within those six weeks, I saw every one of them. I should have known something was going on. Number two, I should have realized that the person was somebody from the office, and I should have stepped back. The attendants were probably busy with something else, and someone probably asked this lady if she would go downstairs and make sure nobody parked in these spots where I parked. That's probably what they told her, and I didn't realize that. After seeing that she wasn't one of the attendants, I should have gone into a kind of "just say hello" mode. When she asked me if I was planning to park there, I should have said "no," or I should have gone back, shut the door and moved to a parking spot. But sometimes things happen so quickly that we don't take time to think.

We should notice changes in our environment and in those we see regularly, and pause for a moment to get the lay of the land. It might be better to take ten steps back, something I did not do that that particular time. When we step back a moment before we respond, we are being respectful of the fact that we are all in this together. When we aren't as careful, we can make others uncomfortable by our quick, and often negative, reaction. As I think about that day, I know that I must give it to God and apologize. I could have apologized to the lady, but I haven't seen her again. I really feel bad about that. I would tell my own children to apologize for that sort of behavior. When something comes up and you are ready to blow your cool, take ten seconds first. You should also visualize yourself taking ten steps backward before you react. Those ten seconds allow us time for a little more perspective, and can help us avoid behavior we may regret.

For the last eleven chapters, I have shared my perspective about life through my experiences in school, religion, and business. I fully understand that what I have said will fail to reach everyone. It is impossible to do so, because we each have our own ways of looking at things. Even so, we put ourselves "out there," through our speech, writing and life ways, sharing our unique perspectives and often disagreeing, even as we understand that we are all in this together. There are a variety of media that enhance our ability to do this: books, papers, Facebook, blogs, twitter, vine, Instagram, and other ways that will emerge after this is published.

I remember a time in 1965 when I was a student at Philander Smith College. We took a class called Institutions. I have been trying to find the old textbook we used in that class. I believe the course and the book dealt with the religious world. That wouldn't be too far off, as religions are types of institutions and share institutional characteristics. I do remember that the course and textbook provided a way to perceive the broad spectrum of what was around us and the types of institutions that would shape our lives.

The key is that the course I just mentioned, as well as others experiences I have had, shaped my life as our experiences and the institutions we find ourselves in shape us all. I came to Little Rock, Arkansas, to go to school. I went into the military, did some travel overseas, worked for the government for fifteen years, and have been in the United Methodist ministry for thirty-four years. I married the summer I graduated from college, and I went into the military that summer as well. Each experience has shaped who I am and how I perceive the world we share.

Each of us has a vision that we hope will lead us to a future of fulfillment and promise. While I can't tell the future, I can say GOD BLESS YOU. I hope you are successful, and that you live a life of love and peace.

## THE END

**For More Information On This And Any Other Book**
**In The Journey Book Series**
**Contact**
**Concise Consulting**
**501-779-0649**
**conciselr@gmail.com**